This book belongs to:

....

Written by Abbey Land

Copyright © 2015 B&H Publishing Group, Nashville, Tennessee

BHPublishingGroup.com

978-1-4336-8728-0

Dewey Decimal Classification: C242.62

Subject Heading: DEVOTIONAL LITERATURE \ JESUS CHRIST

Unless otherwise noted, all Scripture quotations are taken from the Holman
Christian Standard Bible®, Copyright © 1999, 2000, 2002, 2003, 2009
by Holman Bible Publishers. Scriptures marked NIV are taken from Holy Bible,
New International Version®, NIV® Copyright © 1973, 1978, 1984, 2011
by Biblica, Inc. ®. Used by permission. All rights reserved worldwide.

Printed in China

1 2 3 4 5 6 • 19 18 17 16 15

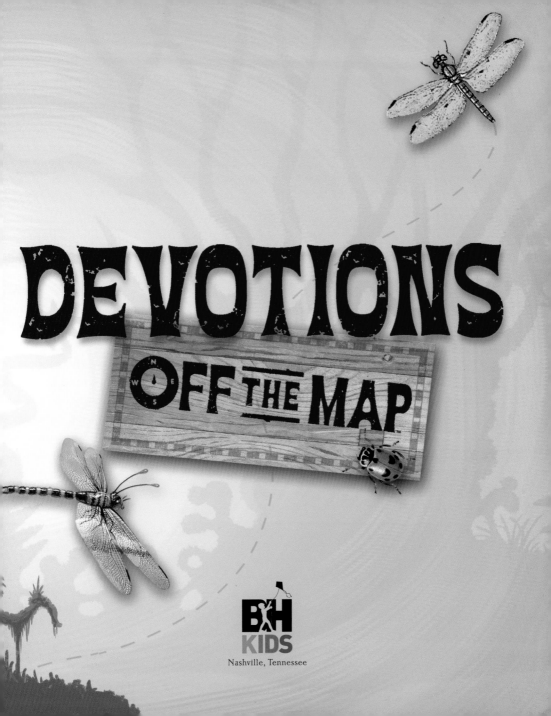

DEVOTIONS

OFF THE MAP

N
W · E
S

B&H
KIDS
Nashville, Tennessee

Dear Parents,

God has an amazing plan for your children's futures, and these fifty-two devotions will help them map out their journeys. Don't be afraid to go off the map this year! Each week you will find a devotion, Scriptures, prayer, discussion questions, and activities to help your kids face uncharted territory with faith and courage.

As your children read their weekly devotions, they'll learn more about following the ultimate Guide, Jesus. You can share the lessons as a family and discuss preparing for the challenges ahead, getting along with fellow travelers, and staying focused when faced with detours and obstacles.

There's a lot to learn while traveling through life. Help your kids to know what direction to go by getting into the Scriptures and on the right path.

Each devotion offers the following sections to guide your study time. Are you ready? The journey awaits!

THE OVERLOOK This brief description lets your child know what will be discussed in the devotion. Looking for a specific topic? You can glance at this section and quickly know what you'll be reading about.

THIS IS THE WAY Each devotion provides one key Bible verse and extra scripture references to take devotion time further. Some days you and your child may want to dig in and see what else the Bible says about that devotion's topic. Searching for more verses is a great way to show kids that the Bible has a lot more to say than you can find in one devotion.

LESSONS FROM THE TANGLED TREEHOUSE

Here's where the devotions come in. These are easy to read and explore lots of situations and challenges your child might find familiar. Plus, the lesson supports the key verse for that devotion, showing readers that God's Word is always there to guide us.

SHADY GROVE PRAYER

These are simple yet effective prayers that kids can pray alone or with the family. As your child becomes more comfortable, he may choose to add his own thoughts or pray his own prayer.

FIELD STUDY

Field Study includes four discussion questions that often begin with *why, how, when,* or *where.* These questions are not quick yes-or-no responses. Instead they ask kids to share what they think about a subject, so there's no pressure to provide the right answer. Listen to your children's responses, and be sure to affirm their ideas and opinions when you can. This is an opportunity to guide your children and understand their thoughts as they begin to work through different subjects and topics.

WALKING TO BOULDER BRIDGE

The goal of this section is to help your child apply what he's read about in the devotion. You'll find different activities, service projects, simple crafts, or discussion ideas. Most activities should take about five to ten minutes to complete, but they reinforce important concepts and encourage kids to keep walking on the right path throughout the week.

Prepping for Your Journey

The journey is about to begin—are you ready? Do you have the right supplies? The necessary know-how? What do you need to pack? It's time to prepare for the challenges ahead, and this chapter will show you how. Read on to discover how to prep and what to pack for your adventure. Soon, you'll be ready for the next journey God has planned for you.

Prepping for Your Journey:
A COMMUNICATION PLAN

In this devotion, you'll learn about the importance of prayer.

Pray constantly.
-1 Thessalonians 5:17

1 Chronicles 16:11   Psalm 4:1
Psalm 145:18   Luke 18:1
Colossians 4:2

You have an exciting journey ahead! Before you set out into uncharted territory, it's time to prepare for your journey.

What's the first thing you need to do? Before you pack your supplies or chart your course, you have an important task to complete—praying! It's time for you to go off the map and into the plan God created and designed just for you. So the more you communicate with God, the more you will know His plan for you.

God will always be there to listen when you pray to Him. You know how sometimes your mom can't stop and talk to you because she's making dinner? Or how your friend can't talk on the phone after 8 p.m.? You will never have that problem with God. All hours of the night or day, 24/7, 52 weeks, 365 days a year, you can communicate with Him.

Do you ever struggle with what to say to God? If you need help praying, here's a good format to follow. First, praise and worship God for who He is and what He has done. Next comes supplication. This is when you ask God to supply your needs or requests. Then thanksgiving is the time during prayer when you thank God for your many blessings. Intercession is next, and this is when you intercede, or pray, specifically for friends and others who need encouragement and help. Finally, confession is a time that allows you to tell God things you've done wrong. If you confess your sins, Jesus will forgive you of those sins.

God wants to hear from you and spend time with you. You can pray to Him while sitting in church or standing on the ball field. You can pray silently, or you can choose to pray out loud. God hears your prayers no matter how you pray them. Make prayer an important part of each day's journey.

Dear God,

You are amazing! Help me to see people who are lost and need help. Show me how to talk to people who need You. Thank You for Jesus and His death on the cross for me. I pray for my family and friends to know they need to talk with You. I want to be a good example to everyone I meet each day.

Amen

???

- How do you think praying affects your relationship with God?
- Why is it important to pray every day and not just when you are needing something?
- When should you quit praying?
- Can you name some times when you've prayed and God has answered your prayers?

1. Grab a washable marker and write each of the following words on a different finger on the same hand: Adore, Supply, Thank, Intercede, Confess. (If you don't want to write on your hand, trace your hand on a piece of paper and cut it out.)

2. Gather your family together, and ask them to pray with you. Talk about the different parts of prayer.

3. Pray. Ask God to prepare you for the journey you are on.

4. Study the parts of prayer, and be familiar with all five parts before the ink washes off your hand.

Prepping for Your Journey:
LIGHTING THE LAMP

The Bible is more than just a book! In this devotion, you'll learn about the importance of reading God's Word.

You are leaving tomorrow on a trip. You aren't sure exactly where you'll be going. You do know you won't have electricity, running water, or any way to call home. What basic things do you need to pack? Clothes, bottled water, a sleeping bag, and maybe a flashlight. Wait—definitely a flashlight. Have you ever tried to walk around at night with no way to see? You would have bruises on your legs from bumping into things. A flashlight helps you know where to go and see what's up ahead.

In Psalm 119:105, the Bible is compared to a lamp and a light because it can show you which way to go. Sounds like a must-have item for the journey you are beginning! How does a Bible help you? The Bible is full of commands from God, truths about how much He loves us, and information about the many people who lived before you. The Bible also chronicles the life of Jesus Christ, the ultimate example of how you should live your life.

> Your word is
> a lamp for my feet
> and a light on
> my path.
> -Psalm 119:105

Deuteronomy 11:18
Proverbs 3:12
John 1:1
Hebrews 4:12
Revelation 1:3

In short, the Bible is truth. It's your textbook for life. It doesn't change, and it's never outdated. Anybody can pick up the Bible, read it, and learn from its words because the Bible is full of answers. Are you sad? The Bible gives hope for the future. Are you angry? The Bible provides ways to calm down. Are you confused? The Bible can give you directions. Are you unsure about an important decision? The Bible helps you recognize what is most important in life. Wow—that's some flashlight!

Why should you pack a Bible on this journey? The Bible lights your way and shows you which way to turn. Stumbling through the dark is never fun, especially if you end up on the wrong path. Let God's Word light your way instead.

Dear God,

Thank You for the Bible and its instructions for living life the way You want me to. Honor the time I spend studying Your Word, and help me to use what I learn in my life. Help me to remember how important it is to study my Bible and make it a priority on my journey.

Amen

- If everything in the Bible happened long ago, why is it still important to us today?

- How long will what's found in the Bible be important in your life?

- When is the best time of day to study your Bible?

- When you read from the Bible, what should you do about what you've read?

1. Choose a verse from the Bible that you really like. Maybe you already have a favorite!

2. Ask God to help you learn your favorite verse.

3. Choose a way to study the verse you pick. Write it on an index card or on the front of a school folder.

4. Recite your favorite verse from memory to a friend or family member.

Prepping for Your Journey:
STUDY THE MAP

Have you got a good memory? In this devotion, you'll learn about the importance of memorizing Scripture.

If you read the directions to a destination one time then try to follow them without checking again, how easy would it be for you to find your way? What if you studied a map and read the directions twice? The more you read them, the more familiar you would become with them. Before long, you might realize that you'd studied the map so much that you had it memorized. Then you would feel confident that you could reach your destination. Even if you lost the map and your cell phone, or had no cell service, you would still know which way to go because the map and directions were safe in your mind.

On your journey through life, you have a special map to help you get where you're going. It doesn't look like a typical map with directions to get you from one place to another though. The map you need is called your Bible, and the more of it you have in your head, the better. You may think it's enough to have a Bible (or a Bible app) close by. But you never know when you might need to recall a verse from the Bible. In preparation for your journey, you should challenge yourself to memorize Scripture.

When you memorize words from the Bible, you can share verses easily with others. And memorizing and reciting verses will allow you to think more deeply about the words and their meanings. The more you think about those verses, the more a part of your life they become.

How do you decide what verses to memorize? A good place to start might be a Scripture that helps you share the gospel with other kids.

That way, you are prepared to share the verses you've read with others who need to hear God's Word, even if you're at the lake, on a hike, or anywhere else where your Bible app won't be much help.

The more you study your map, the more verses you can add to memory. The more verses you have memorized, the more you will be able to share your faith with both friends and strangers. Plus you'll remember which direction you're headed yourself. You won't get lost along the journey, and you'll be prepared with the words of God whenever you need them.

I have treasured Your word in my heart so that I may not sin against You.
-Psalm 119:11

Jeremiah 15:16   Psalm 119:16
Proverbs 4:20-21   Psalm 1:2
Jude 17

- Name some occasions when memorized Scripture might be helpful to you or others.

- How does memorizing a verse help you understand what it means?

- How should you decide what verses to memorize from the Bible?

- What are some different ways you can memorize Scripture?

1. Ask your parents which verses they have memorized and which ones mean a lot to them.

2. Talk to your parents about times they've recalled scriptures.

3. Work with your parents to memorize one of their favorite verses.

4. Brainstorm different ways to memorize scriptures: Can you sing it? Can you write it down 25 times? What about making a scripture sign over your mirror?

Dear God,

Thank You for the Bible, Your Holy Word. Thank You for the wisdom and direction it gives me to use in my life. Help me to understand what the Bible says and how to use it to make decisions. Please help me memorize verses that will guide me and the people I meet.

Amen

Prepping for Your Journey:
PROTECT YOURSELF

We all get scared sometimes. In this devotion, you'll learn about praying for God's protection.

Starting out on a journey can be scary. You don't know what's ahead. You think you know what to expect, but until you take a step, you really don't. Maybe you'll do something exciting that you never dreamed of doing. But maybe you'll experience fear, temptations, or disappointments too. The more prepared you are for your journey, the better you'll be able to handle whatever comes your way, even the difficult things.

Do you know what the armor of God is? No, it isn't a heavy metal suit you can wear that probably weighs more than you do! The armor of God is found in Ephesians 6, and it's what you need to face temptation and difficult times. Where will this temptation come from? Reread Ephesians 6:11 to see. The Devil will tempt you, and the armor will protect you. When you pray for God's protection, it doesn't mean you won't be attacked. It does mean that God will give you strength to face each difficulty and temptation.

Each piece of God's armor provides a different kind of protection. When you pray, ask Him for the belt of truth, the breastplate of righteousness, the shield of faith, the helmet of Salvation, and the sword of the Spirit—God's Word. The pieces of physical armor are reminders of things you should have when facing each day. When you wake up each morning and prepare for your journey, pray for the armor of God. Name each piece and what it stands for. Once you've prayed, you are better prepared to face the day. You can't see the future, but God knows what will happen. When you face fears and temptations, God and His armor are there to protect you.

Put on the full armor of God so that you can stand against the tactics of the Devil.
–Ephesians 6:11

Ephesians 6:13   Ephesians 6:14
Ephesians 6:15   Ephesians 6:16
Ephesians 6:17

Dear God,

You are the ultimate protector!
Thank You for watching out
for me and giving Your armor
to keep me safe. Help me to
remember that no matter what
I face, You will be by my side.
I praise You for what You've
done for me and will do for me
in the future.
Amen

- **What kind of tactics do you think the Devil uses to tempt you to sin?**
- **Why do you think it is important to pray for the armor of God to protect you?**
- **How do you think you will feel once you've prayed for the armor of God?**
- **Spend thirty seconds talking about what fears you have about your future. Now spend sixty seconds talking about how God takes care of you.**

1. Gather some art supplies: markers, paints, colored pencils, crayons, and paper.

2. Read the Bible verses on page 15 and use them to design a picture of the armor of God.

3. Label each piece with its name and the verse that describes the piece.

4. Place your drawing somewhere that's visible to you in the morning. Use the picture as a reminder to pray for the armor of God.

Prepping for Your Journey:
WALKING WISELY

After months of planning and preparing, my family of six, my parents, and two friends are ready for our trip. That's ten people traveling together! We have our passports, our luggage, hotel reservations, and plane tickets ready to go. The packing list has been checked and rechecked. Everything we think we need is with us, but we still don't know exactly what to expect. You see, my family is getting on a boat for seven days and sailing to places we've never been before. We are going to a place that is sunny and warm when it's the middle of winter where we live. How will we get around a boat we've never been on before? Where will we eat our meals? What trip excursions will we choose?

The good news is that after talking with several of my friends who have been on this cruiseship, I've learned some tips. They told us exactly where to go to make dinner reservations once we get on the boat, the best places to go on excursions, and the best way to move around the ship. I'm learning from what others have experienced and using what I've learned to make decisions. That's called wisdom.

You're on a journey too. Each day you wake up, you have to make choices. How will you treat your parents and your friends? What will you do this afternoon? What will you choose to do when others treat you wrong? Proverbs 2:6 gives you the answer. "The Lord gives wisdom." Aren't sure which way to turn? Ask God. Having trouble deciding how to respond to a friend who hurt your feelings? Ask God what you should say and do.

Once you've been through any experience, you learn from it. After I return from my trip, I will have tips and ideas of how to travel next time. I'm going to write them down so I don't forget what I've learned! As you make choices and decisions, consider keeping a journal to write down your thoughts. When you read your Bible, you might have questions or a verse you want to remember. You can write those things down in your journal. Prayer is important too. Have you ever written down your prayers or what you've prayed about? It's an excellent way to look back and see how God has answered prayers.

Your age doesn't matter when it comes to wisdom. The more you learn about how to live a godly life, the more wisdom you have. Read and study the Bible to discover what God says to do in each situation. With reading Scripture and prayer, you'll be on your way to making decisions that will allow you to walk wisely through your journey.

For the LORD gives wisdom; from His mouth come knowledge and understanding.
–Proverbs 2:6

1 Corinthians 10:6   Matthew 4:4
1 Corinthians 10:11   Psalm 119:11

Dear God,

Thank You for Your guidance. Thank You for the Bible and for prayer. Help me to use them to gain more and more wisdom and to live a life that is pleasing to You.

Amen

- Why is it a good idea to write down prayer requests?
- What are some ways you might use a journal when reading your Bible?
- Read Proverbs 2:6 again. Who do you think the Lord gives wisdom to?
- Why is wisdom important?

1. Buy, find, or make a simple journal to write in. You can use an inexpensive spiral notebook or just staple together some pieces of paper.

2. Find a way to attach a pen to the journal using yarn or string.

3. Choose a special place to keep your Bible and journal together where you can reach them easily.

4. Work at using your Bible and journal together and keeping them in the same place so they will be ready for your next journey.

Prepping for Your Journey:
DOING YOUR PART

In this devotion, you'll learn about how each person is an important part of the church.

For as the body is one and has many parts, and all the parts of that body, though many, are one body—so also is Christ.
–1 Corinthians 12:12

Romans 12:5   1 Corinthians 12:27
1 Corinthians 14:26   Ephesians 4:12

We have so much to do to get ready for this trip. Maybe we should stay home from church today," Gena's mom suggested. "I just don't think I can get it all done before we have to leave."

Gena's dad looked up from his breakfast. "You're right about one thing. You can't get it all done, but we're still going to church today," he said.

Gena and her brother were confused. "Dad, what do you mean? You just said you agreed with Mom. She can't get everything packed."

Gena's dad smiled and said, "Exactly. Your mom can't do it all, but we can all work together to get things ready to go. In fact, we should have offered to help her much sooner. Packing for our trip isn't a good excuse for skipping church." Mom began to make assignments, and in no time all the luggage was packed and everyone was dressed and ready for church.

In the car on the way to church, Gena's family was listening to a Christian radio station when a song about being the body of Christ came on. Gena said, "I don't get it. Why is this song calling the church 'a body'?" (1 Corinthians 12:24)

Gena's dad explained, "One reason we go to church is to worship God together, and each person is a different but important part of the body of Christ. We can work together to serve God in different ways. Some people teach Sunday school or rock babies in the nursery. Others greet visitors or help keep the church clean. We all have different ways to help. Our family goes to church because we want to be a part of the body. We want to worship God with other believers. When we make it a priority to go to church and do our part, we get to serve God together and build relationships with other members too.

"Think about it, Gena. When we worked together to get packed this morning, the job was much easier. It's the same with church. We can each do our part, and together we can show God that He is our number-one priority."

Dear God,

Sometimes it feels like I'm too tired to get up for church. Help me to want to worship You and to please You no matter where I am. Show me how to be an important part of the body of Christ too.
Amen

- Read further into 1 Corinthians 12. What else do you learn about being a member of a church?

- Why is going to church and being involved important?

- What are some excuses people use about why they can't go to church?

- How can you serve at church?

1. Sometimes getting to church can be rushed. Ask your parent how you can help things go smoothly on Sunday morning.

2. Work with a parent to develop a "Smooth Sunday Sailing" plan.

3. Keep the plan simple. Review the steps you make several times. You can even make a sign as a reminder for the family.

4. Share the "Smooth Sunday Sailing" plan with other families, and challenge them to make church a priority in their lives too.

Prepping for Your Journey:
TRAINING WITH THE BEST

In this devotion, you'll learn what a mentor is and how to choose one.

When I was young, my Mimi and Papaw lived in the country. On our way to visit them, my family would take a winding road through vine covered trees, small hills, and farms. I knew that when I arrived, I could ask Mimi to tell me stories. She had studied the Bible her whole life, and I would ask her questions about what different things in the Bible meant. She would watch me as I pretended to preach about John 3:16 to various cows that grazed in the pasture. She was often writing in a weekly calendar book, and whenever I visited, I would open it and read about her different prayer requests for each day.

My Mimi and Papaw eventually decided to move into the city. I would stop by, and she would make me a snack. We would sit around the kitchen table and talk about life. Mimi always had good advice, and she would provide verses and examples from the Bible to explain what she taught me. Mimi had learned a lot, and she was good at sharing her wisdom. I knew if I had questions about something, I could always go to her.

One generation will declare Your works to the next and will proclaim Your mighty acts.
–Psalm 145:4

Psalm 71:16
Psalm 78:6
2 Timothy 2:1-2
Titus 2:2
Titus 2:3

I didn't realize it at the time, but Mimi was my mentor. A mentor is someone you look up to and who can help train you because she has already been on the journey that you're on now. A mentor provides advice and help.

Do you have a mentor? Maybe you do but you just didn't realize what to call him or her! If you don't, pray and ask God to help you find a mentor, someone you can trust to give you advice that comes from his or her experience and what the Bible says to do. Look for someone who is active in church, studies the Bible, and is older than you. As you grow up, mentors can help you choose how to prepare for the journey ahead. They've already been on that journey, and they can train you to choose the path that pleases God. You've got a big future ahead of you, so train with the best!

Dear God,

Thank You, God, for putting people in my life to encourage me as I grow up. Sometimes I may not know what choice to make. Thank You for providing me help to know what to do. It's another way You show the plans You have for me.
Amen

???

- Why is it important to have a mentor?
- What are some things you might ask a mentor for advice about?
- How is a mentor different than a teacher?
- When would you be considered a mentor to others?

1. Do you have a mentor? If not, pray about asking someone to be your mentor.

2. Talk to your parents about who you want to ask to be your mentor.

3. Ask that person to be your mentor.

4. Discuss with a parent when and how often you would like to meet with your mentor. (If you already have a mentor, write a quick note of thanks to him or her.)

Prepping for Your Journey:
A LESSON IN LOST LUGGAGE

After a crazy plane ride that landed on a very bumpy gravel runway, the family mission team to Haiti finally arrived at its destination. Kelsie commented, "Who knew you didn't have to have a paved runway?" All the families nodded in agreement. They were all looking forward to their mission-trip adventure.

The luggage was being unloaded and given to each family. But as the last bag was unloaded, Julia looked worried. "Are you sure that's the last bag?" she asked. Tim, the man in charge of the trip, said, "Yep. Looks like that's it!"

Uh oh. Julia looked upset as she explained that her bag didn't make it. The team didn't have time for Julia to shop for new clothes because they had to quickly get on a bus to make it to their final destination. But her friend Kelsie whispered to her mom and then said, "Julia, you can wear some of my clothes! We share at home anyway!"

Julia looked a little surprised, "Are you sure? Didn't you bring just enough for the trip?"

Kelsie responded, "We can always wash the clothes out at night and wear them again the next day. Besides, with no air conditioning, wet clothes may feel good!" Julia and her mom seemed relieved, and the team got on the bus excited to see how they were going to serve others in Haiti.

Kelsie is a great example of a cheerful giver—and that's what God asks us to be! There are many different ways to give. God makes it clear in the Bible that you are to give a tithe, or 10 percent, of the money you've earned back to Him through your church. An offering is giving more

How do you feel about giving? In this devotion, you'll learn about giving cheerfully.

than 10 percent of what you've earned, and these offerings can be about more than money— like how Kelsie gave some of her clothes to Julia. You can offer God your time and talents too. Whether you're giving money or time, God wants you to give willingly and cheerfully and not just because you think you are required to do so. He wants you to give because it honors Him.

Each person should do as he has decided in his heart–not reluctantly or out of necessity, for God loves a cheerful giver.
–2 Corinthians 9:7

Deuteronomy 15:10   1 Chronicles 29:9
Proverbs 11:25   Malachi 3:10
Romans 12:8

- How could Kelsie have responded differently to Julia's situation?
- Why do you think God loves a cheerful giver?
- What are some ways you can give to God that won't cost you any money?
- How old do you think you should be when you begin to tithe?

1. Think about what it means to be cheerful when you give.
2. Ask your parent for an envelope, and draw a smiley face on it.
3. If you have a bank or wallet where you keep your money, put the envelope near the bank.
4. The next time you tithe, use the envelope as a reminder of how God wants you to give. Remember, giving can be about more than money.

Dear God,

Thank You for giving Your Son to die on the cross for my sins. Thank You for the opportunity to give back to You. I want to be a cheerful giver. Please show me how to honor You through giving.
Amen

Prepping for Your Journey:
ARE YOU READY?

One day, my eight-year-old neighbor Kyle came over to my house and saw all the crosses I had hanging on my wall. He looked at the crosses then looked at me and said, "Why do you have a bunch of T's on your wall?" I wasn't sure what he meant at first, but then I realized he wasn't familiar with someone hanging crosses on the wall. He saw the crosses as lowercase letter T's, not as a symbol of Jesus' sacrifice for all people's sins.

I couldn't believe my neighbor didn't recognize a cross. Doesn't everyone know what the cross represents? I thought for sure everyone on my street was a Christian. When Kyle asked me what the crosses stood for, I struggled with my words. I didn't want to confuse him, but I knew I needed to tell him about Jesus. I guessed that his parents must not attend church or had never taken Kyle there. I didn't know where to start when explaining who Jesus is to someone who didn't know anything about Him.

Have you ever had to explain Jesus and the cross to someone who had never heard of Jesus before? Are you ready to do that if someone wants to know more about Him? You may be like I was and just assume everybody you know could tell you that Jesus died on the cross to save people from their sins. The truth is, some people don't know about Jesus.

Get ready.
In this devotion,
you'll learn about
telling others
about Jesus.

Maybe you are homeschooled or go to a private Christian school, so you don't think you run into people who don't know Jesus. You still go to the mall, to the ballpark, and to the movies. You may walk past a person who wonders why you have a shirt with the letter "T" on it. What should you do if someone stops and talks with you? According to 1 Peter 3:15, God wants you to be ready to explain the hope Jesus offers to anyone who asks.

Along your journey, someone may stop you to ask about Jesus. Be ready to share His truth with anyone who may ask. Think about how you would explain who Jesus is to someone who has never heard of Him. Are you ready?

Isaiah 6:8   Jeremiah 1:7
Mark 1:38   Luke 10:2
Romans 10:15

Honor the Messiah
as Lord in your hearts.
Always be ready to give
a defense to anyone who
asks you for a reason for
the hope that is in you.
–1 Peter 3:15

Dear God,

You are the Master of the universe. You created all things, and everything You created is good. I want to be ready to tell others about You. Give me the words to say to those who need to hear about You.

Amen

- Why is it important to be ready to talk about Jesus?
- How would you explain who Jesus is to someone who has never heard of Him before?
- What does the symbol of the cross represent?
- According to 1 Peter 3:15, what should you explain to others?

1. Ask a friend, parent, or sibling to help you practice telling the truth about Jesus.

2. Choose a few different places you might meet people who don't know Jesus, such as a baseball game, a friend's house, or camp.

3. Practice telling your friend about Jesus in the different settings you chose.

4. Talk with your friend about how it felt to share Jesus with someone. Think about how you can become more comfortable with sharing Jesus with others.

Prepping for Your Journey:
LISTEN AND LEARN

In this devotion, you'll learn about listening to the Holy Spirit.

When you are preparing for a trip, there's a lot to be done. Your mom may tell you how many clothes to pack, what the weather will be like where you are going, and how long you'll be away. If you listen closely to what your mom says, you are more likely to pack everything you need. But what if you are so busy thinking about what you plan to do on your trip that you don't hear your mom? You may not realize you need to bring a coat because the temperatures are dropping to 30 degrees that night. Brrrr. Listening is important when packing.

When you're praying, listening is important too. You talk to God; but do you also listen to what God has to say back to you? God provides the Holy Spirit to guide you. Once you become a Christian, the Holy Spirit lives inside of you, and He speaks truth. If you ask for help, the Holy Spirit will guide you. You need to listen to what He has to say.

So what if you don't know how to listen? The best way to listen is to stop talking. Being quiet can be a challenge, especially for those of us who like to talk. Maybe you've played the quiet game before, and you never seem to win. But with practice, you can learn how to be a better listener. When you pray, allow some time to just be quiet at the end of the prayer. Keep thinking about God and listening for the Holy Spirit. The more you stop and listen to God and His Holy Spirit, the more you'll learn about making good decisions that allow you to walk in truth no matter where your journey takes you.

> When the Spirit of truth comes, He will guide you into all the truth. For He will not speak on His own, but He will speak whatever He hears. He will also declare to you what is to come.
> –John 16:13

Isaiah 11:2
Isaiah 11:12

John 15:26
Acts 5:32
1 John 5:6

Dear God,

Thank You for the Holy Spirit. Sometimes it's hard to listen, but help me to be quiet so I can hear what the Holy Spirit has to say. Please remind me that I can trust the Holy Spirit to guide me.

Amen

- **What is the Holy Spirit?**
- **How can the Holy Spirit help you?**
- **Do you have a hard time listening? Why is it important not to talk the whole time during prayer but to listen as well?**
- **When does the Holy Spirit live in you?**

1. Seek out a quiet place in your house.

2. Ask God for help with a difficult decision.

3. Spend a few moments in silence, listening for the Holy Spirit to guide you.

4. Thank God for His help. You may not get an immediate answer to your prayer request or need. Be patient.

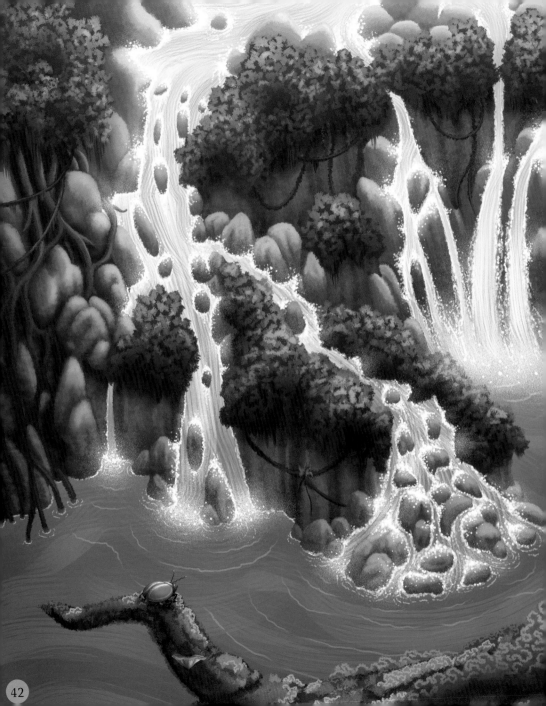

Following Your Guide

How can you get somewhere if you don't really know the way? Meet your Guide, Jesus. He will be with you every step of your journey. Who is this Guide? He's dependable, and He has all the answers. Jesus will never take you down the wrong path, and in this chapter, you'll learn all about how to follow Him.

The more you know about your Guide, the more you'll trust Him to lead you on this journey.

Following Your Guide:
THE ONLY SINLESS MAN

Only one person has walked this earth without ever sinning. Read on to discover more about this man called Jesus.

Think about the many different kinds of sins. How many sins do you think one typical person commits a day? What about a week? Can you imagine adding up how many sins a person commits in an entire year? Let's do the math. If a person sinned 5 times a day x 7 days in a week x 52 weeks in a year, that equals 1,820 sins a year. That's a lot!

So, what is sin? Sin includes actions, words, and thoughts that aren't pleasing to God. Sin happens when you choose to do something you know you shouldn't do. If you get angry with your mom and talk disrespectfully to her, that's sin. If you let your eyes peek at your friend's answers during a test, that's sin. And the time you shared that rumor about the new kid on the bus? That was sin too. Sin also happens when you don't do something you know you should do, like the time you chose not to forgive your little brother.

The Bible talks a lot about sin. Every person who lives in this world sins. Only one person who has walked the earth has done so without sinning. Does that sound impossible? Read 2 Corinthians 5:21. Do you know who this verse is talking about? The "He" at the beginning of the verse is talking about God. God made the "One" named Jesus, and Jesus has never sinned! Wow! Can you imagine? He has never broken any laws God commanded. No lying, no cheating, no jealousy or disrespect. The Bible tells us why Jesus didn't sin—He did it for us, for you and me.

He became the sacrifice, or replacement, for you on the cross. He died so you do not have to suffer eternally. Even though Jesus never sinned, He was punished for all the sins people have committed. He took the blame, and He was crucified on the cross. He died for you, a sinner. Jesus died for you, so make it your goal to live like Him. Being sinless is impossible, but working hard to live a life that makes God happy is possible.

He made the One who did not know sin to be sin for us, so that we might become the righteousness of God in Him.
–2 Corinthians 5:21

Mark 14:55
John 19:4

Hebrews 4:15
1 Peter 2:22

1 John 3:5

Dear God,

I know I'm a sinner. Please forgive me and help me recognize my sins. Show me how to do better at saying no to sin when I am tempted. Amen

- Why is it important for you to remember that Jesus is sinless?

- How should you react when you are accused of doing something wrong that you never did? Think about how Jesus was punished for something He didn't do.

- How can you choose to sin less?

- You probably feel bad when you sin. Why do you think you still sin again?

- What can you do to help you make better choices?

1. Find a dry-erase board or a mirror (with a parent's permission). Use a dry-erase marker to list a few sins you've committed today. Maybe you've been mean to your brother or disrespectful to a parent. The sin could be you've been lazy and not gotten your chores done. You don't have to show what you've written to anyone else.

2. Now, erase the words you wrote until you can't see them anymore.

3. When you ask for forgiveness, God forgives you of your sins and forgets them just like you erased them from the board. Only God has this power!

Following Your Guide:
YOUR GUIDE FOR HOLINESS

When you travel to a different country, it's a good idea to be familiar with the etiquette of people living in the area. That way you'll know how to act to be respectful of the local customs. For example, in many Asian countries, it is polite to remove your shoes when you enter a person's home. You might even be provided slippers to wear. Once when I traveled to a country where I didn't speak the language, I had a guide who helped me communicate with people. She helped me know when it was okay to keep my shoes on and when I needed to remove them.

When God was talking with Moses in Exodus 3:5, He told Moses to take off his shoes too. But it was for a different reason. God said to Moses, "Remove the sandals from your feet, for the place where you are standing is holy ground." When something is declared holy, it is set apart for God's glory. Jesus is holy because Jesus is God. When Jesus' mother, Mary, was told of Jesus' birth, the angel said, "The Holy Spirit will come upon you, and the power of the Most High will overshadow you.

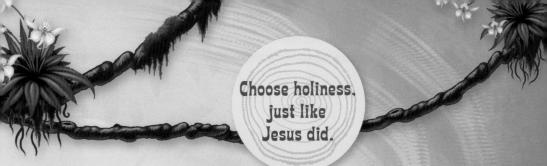

Choose holiness, just like Jesus did.

Therefore, the holy One to be born will be called the Son of God" (Luke 1:35). Jesus has never sinned and will always be holy.

God made the ground holy when He was talking with Moses, and He wants you to want to be holy too. In 1 Peter 1:14–16, Peter writes, "As obedient children, do not be conformed to the desires of your former ignorance. But as the One who called you is holy, you also are to be holy in all your conduct; for it is written, Be holy, because I am holy."

When you love God, you want to please Him. When your actions and words honor God, you can be holy too. You will never be perfect like Jesus, but you can choose to do your best to live a holy life. Jesus is familiar with struggles, temptation, and difficult situations, and He is the perfect guide for how to life a life that is holy and pleasing to God, no matter what country you're in.

"I know who You are–the Holy One of God!" –Mark 1:24

Exodus 3:5   Acts 3:14
1 Corinthians 9:2   Hebrews 2:11
Hebrews 13:12

Dear God,

You are holy and worthy of all praise. Thank You for Jesus and His example of how to live my life. I want to live a life that is pleasing to You too. Help me to choose to be holy and honor You. Amen

- Who do you think can be holy?

- Why should you want to be holy?

- What does being holy look like? If you choose to be holy, does it change what you say, where you go, or what you do?

- Why is it important to recognize that Jesus is holy?

1. Make a list of songs you know that include the word *holy*.

2. Choose a song off your list to either listen to or sing.

3. Think about the meaning of the words as the song plays.

4. Challenge yourself to think about ways you can choose to live a holy life.

Following Your Guide:
JESUS KNOWS IT ALL

Jesus knows everything. Yep, everything!

What's your favorite subject in school? Whatever it is, you probably know a lot about it. For example, if your favorite subject is science, you've probably studied plants. If you were deserted with no map for help, you might be able to identify which plants are safe to eat and which aren't. You probably know that poison ivy forms three-leaf clusters, so you don't go near it. As the old saying goes, "Leaves of three, let it be!" But no matter how much you study plants, it would be impossible for you to know all there is to know about them. God made way too many plants for you to know everything!

Knowing everything isn't a problem for Jesus. He is omniscient (say it like this: om-NISH-uhnt). This means Jesus is all-knowing. He knows every single thing about you. Not only that, but Jesus knows what you are thinking as well. Did your sister spill the cereal on the counter earlier, blame it on you, and get away with it? Even if you didn't say it out loud,

> But perceiving their thoughts, Jesus said, "Why are you thinking evil things in your hearts?"
> –Matthew 9:4

Matthew 12:25
Luke 6:8
Luke 9:47
John 16:30
John 21:17

if you thought, *she's such a brat!* Jesus knows. He knows every thought you have ever had.

So how is it possible for Jesus to know everything? God, Jesus, and the Holy Spirit are three in one, the Trinity. This means Jesus knows you, because God knows you. He made you, and Matthew 10:30 says He even knows the number of hairs on your head!

Understanding that Jesus is omniscient means you recognize Jesus knows you—what you do, what you feel, what you think. If you want to serve Him, He knows. If you are worshipping Him in the middle of class, He knows, even if your friends around you don't know what you are doing. Are you trying hard to trust God even though all your friends seem angry at you right now? Jesus knows and cares. You can trust Him. Who better as a guide for you through life than Someone who knows all things?

Dear God,

You know everything, and that is amazing! You even know all my thoughts. Help me to think thoughts and do things that honor You, even when no one else knows what I'm doing. Thank You for loving me when I don't deserve to be loved by You.

Amen

- What does the word *omniscient* mean?
- Who do you know who is omniscient?
- Why is it important for you to recognize that Jesus knows everything about the world and everything about you?
- How does recognizing Jesus is omniscient affect what you think and do?

1. Think about your thoughts over the past twenty-four hours.

2. Evaluate your thoughts. This means you think about whether your thoughts have been good and positive thoughts or negative and hurtful.

3. Come up with a plan to change your thoughts the next time they aren't the kind of thinking that pleases Jesus.

4. Ask God to help you remember He is omniscient, and ask for His help in choosing thoughts, actions, and words that please God.

Following Your Guide:
THE ONE WITH ALL THE POWER

Jesus has power over all things.

Every year, my family takes a trip to the mountains of North Carolina. One year, a rock slide had covered the road we take to reach our mountain getaway. We had to take a detour, and it took more than an hour just to get around the rocks! The rocks were being moved as quickly as possible, but the workers and machinery could only clear the road one rock at a time.

When my family returned to the mountains the next year, the road was clear. All the rocks had slowly been removed, and a new retaining wall had been built. The power of men, women, and machines made it possible for people to finally travel the road again. My family couldn't help but think that it would have been cleared a lot quicker if someone had been able to use super powers. Someone like Jesus, maybe?

Jesus' power is far, far greater than any other person or machine on earth. He is omnipotent, which means all powerful. With one command, He could stop a tornado or move a mountain if He chose to do so. In Mark 4:39, He spoke to the wind and sea, and they obeyed. Who else on earth has ever made the wind and waves obey him? No one else has ever walked the earth with as much power as Jesus has.

When He was crucified, Jesus had the power to remove Himself from the cross. But He stayed. Jesus had the power to take away His own pain and suffering, but He didn't. He made the choice to die on the cross to pay for the sins committed by you and me.

Jesus used His power for good when He was on earth. He brought Lazarus back from death. He healed people of leprosy, a bad skin disease. He helped people walk who were unable to walk just seconds before. He didn't misuse His power in any way. He used it for good. He even conquered death and came back to life. Is there any more amazing example of His power?

He got up, rebuked the wind, and said to the sea, "Silence! Be still!" The wind ceased, and there was a great calm.
–Mark 4:39

Genesis 1:3   Matthew 26:53
Luke 4:14   Colossians 1:17
Hebrews 2:14

Dear God,

You are all powerful. Thank You for Your Son, Jesus, and His power. Help me to remember You are in control of everything. No matter what happens in my life, I know You are the one in power. Amen

- **What does the word *omnipotent* mean?**
- **Why is it important to recognize that Jesus is omnipotent?**
- **How does the power of machines or men with big muscles compare to Jesus' power?**
- **When have you seen Jesus' power at work?**

1. Locate Luke 5:18–26 in your Bible.
2. Read the story about Jesus and the man who couldn't walk.
3. Become familiar with the story, and practice telling the story in your own words.
4. Ask God to help you choose a friend to share the story of Jesus healing the man who couldn't walk. Talk about the power of Jesus.

Following Your Guide:
THE SAVIOR OF THE WORLD

Jesus came to earth to be the Savior of the world.

Imagine your family is backpacking to the top of a mountain, and the family agrees you will carry all the backpacks and supplies. You gather up everyone's gear and start walking. You don't get very far before you fall. You get up and try again. You make it a little farther before you fall down again. The weight is just too much for you. You can't carry everyone's supplies. The weight is more than your body can physically handle.

As you walk through life, your sins can begin to get heavy too. How much does sin weigh? You can't really measure how heavy sin is. But each new sin, each bad choice, makes that load on your back seem harder to handle.

The good news is that Jesus chose to pay the price for every sin that has or will be committed by those who trust in Him. He can take that weight off your shoulders because He chose to take the punishment for your sins. He saved us from those heavy sins even though we didn't deserve to be saved. That's what a Savior does.

No matter how many good things you do on earth, you can't earn your way to heaven. You will still sin, no matter how hard you try not to do it. But Jesus came to save you from your sins, to be the Savior of the world. He chose to pay the price for the sins of all those who walk the earth by dying on a cross. On the third day, He rose again. No other human has died, rose again, and continued to live without dying again.

Jesus is the Savior to all who choose to believe in Him. You have to choose to admit you are a sinner in order for Him to save you. Believe Jesus died on the cross to save you, and confess Him as your Savior. No matter how many backpacks full of sin you have, no matter how heavy your sins feel, Jesus can carry them for you if you'll let Him.

Today a Savior, who is Messiah the Lord, was born for you in the city of David.
–Luke 2:11

Matthew 1:21
Luke 19:10
Acts 13:23

Ephesians 5:23
Philippians 3:20

Dear God,

Forgive me of my sins.
Thank You for sending
Jesus to be the Savior of
the world. Show me ways
to share with others just
how amazing Jesus is.
Amen

- How many people on earth could be the Savior?
- What makes Jesus the Savior?
- How many people can Jesus choose to save?
- Why do you think some people don't believe Jesus is the Savior?

1. Write the letters to the word *Savior* on a piece of paper, one letter of the word per line.

2. Choose something Jesus can save people from that begins with each letter you listed. (If you can't think of a word that begins with that letter, think of a word that has that letter in it.)

3. Ask a parent to help you with your list.

4. Thank Jesus for being Savior over all the things you listed on your paper.

Following Your Guide:
A MESSIAH WHO DELIVERS

There is only one Messiah– Jesus!

The word *Messiah* is used in many songs, but the most popular is probably written by composer George Frideric Handel. He wrote the musical that made its first debut in Dublin, Ireland, in 1742. The music is now heard most often at Christmastime, but Handel originally wrote it for Easter. People were so moved by his work that they stood up, and some even cried! Handel's musical composition covers the prophecies about Jesus: His birth, His life, and His death and resurrection. One of the most famous pieces from Handel's Messiah is the "Hallelujah Chorus." Many people choose to stand out of respect when the chorus is performed.

This guy named Handel lived a long time ago and probably on a different continent than where you live. This might be the first time you've heard of him, but you've probably heard the title *Messiah* used before. Jesus is called the Messiah many times in the Bible. The word means "deliverer."

So why would Jesus be known as the deliverer? A deliverer is someone who rescues others from harm or danger. And that's exactly what the Messiah was to do—rescue us from sin. Before Jesus came to earth, many Old Testament prophecies were made about the coming Messiah. Check out the one in Isaiah 53:4–5. It said that Jesus would come and die in our place, for our sins. All the Old Testament prophecies were made long before Jesus came to earth, but they all came true! Each detail that was described is exactly who Jesus is.

Handel had it right—Jesus definitely deserves a loud hallelujah chorus. You don't have to travel to lots of places to understand who Jesus is and what He has done for you. You can celebrate Jesus as the Messiah right where you are right now. He will deliver you from your sins if you ask Him to do so. He is the Messiah!

But these are written so that you may believe Jesus is the Messiah, the Son of God, and by believing you may have life in His name.
–John 20:31

Matthew 1:16

Matthew 16:16
Matthew 27:17

John 4:25
Acts 17:3

Dear God,

Thank You, thank You for Jesus, the promised Deliverer. Thank You for sending the Messiah. I want to continue to learn and know more about Jesus so I can be more like Him. Amen

- Why is it important for you to know that Jesus is the promised Messiah talked about in Isaiah?

- How do you explain what the word *Messiah* means to someone who doesn't know who Jesus is?

- From what does Jesus deliver people?

- How do you know Jesus is the Messiah?

1. With your parents' help, locate a recording of the "Hallelujah Chorus."

2. Listen to the chorus and follow along with the words if you can.

3. Write down the different titles given to Jesus in the chorus.

4. Think about how you can live your life in a way that others know Jesus is the Messiah.

Following Your Guide:
TRUST ME

You can always trust in Jesus. Always.

The spot on Kaleb's leg didn't look good at all. It was starting to hurt and looked a little swollen. "Are you sure your uncle knows what he's doing?" Kaleb asked his friend Christopher as he watched Christopher's uncle inspect his leg.

Christopher rolled his eyes at Kaleb and said, "Of course he knows what he's doing! He's in medical school. I'm sure he knows all about bee stings."

Kaleb didn't look convinced and asked, "How am I supposed to know I can trust him? I've never seen him go to medical school!"

Uncle Jay smiled at the boys as he reached into the cooler and filled a bag with ice.

"A little ice and prop your leg up for the next few hours, and you should be good to go. I can show you my student i.d. card to prove I'm in medical school if that will make you feel better, Kaleb. I think your afternoon plans of visiting the Rappelling Ravine may need to be rescheduled."

Trust can be a scary thing. Kaleb wasn't sure if he could trust Uncle Jay because he didn't know much about him. It's important to make good decisions about who we can trust and who we can't.

So how do you know you can trust Jesus? In John 14:6, Jesus tells us He IS the truth. Anything the Bible said He would do while on earth, He did. The Bible says to trust in Jesus, and when you do, He will direct you and show you the way to go. You may not be able to see Jesus and physically touch Him, but you can choose to trust that He is alive and that He loves you.

Although Kaleb didn't know much about Uncle Jay, you can know a lot about Jesus! Read your Bible. Learn more about who Jesus is and what He has done for you. You can trust Him to lead you when you ask for His help!

Jesus told him, "I am the way, the truth, and the life. No one comes to the Father except through Me." –John 14:6

Psalm 3:4   1 Chronicles 16:11
John 14:1   Romans 1:18
1 Peter 2:1-5

Dear God,

Sometimes it's hard to know whom I can trust. Thank You for making Jesus the Truth—the One I can trust with anything. I know that no matter what I am going through, I can trust Jesus to guide me. He loves me and will never point me in the wrong direction. Amen

???

- Why is it difficult to trust people sometimes?
- Why is it important to trust Jesus?
- How has Jesus shown you that you can trust Him?
- What are some situations you might have when you need to remember to trust Jesus?

1. Invite a parent, sibling, or friend to complete the activity with you and serve as your guide.

2. Use a scarf, headband, or bandana to cover your eyes.

3. Ask your designated guide to hold your hands and lead you through an area in your home or outside. Pay attention to how difficult it may be to trust your guide to keep you safe.

4. Remove your eye covering. Think about your experience. Do you think it is easier or more difficult to trust Jesus to be your guide?

Following Your Guide:
WHO'S IN CHARGE?

Jesus is over everything and everyone.

Who's in charge here? I wondered. I was confused. I was in a new country, thousands of miles from my home. In America, you have the president of the United States. Now, I was in a different country, and I wasn't sure who was in charge. I did some research, and I was still confused! Instead of a president, this country has a queen and a prime minister. The queen is called the Head of the State and the prime minister is called the Head of Government. The queen is born into her role, but the prime minister is voted into his role. The country had a government called a Parliament, but I was used to a Congress. See how I was confused?

Do you ever wonder who is in charge too? Sure, there are government officials in charge of making and enforcing laws in our country. Teachers make the rules at school, and parents rule the roost at home. But ultimately, who is *really* in charge? According to Philippians 2:11, Jesus is Lord of all.

> **Every tongue should confess that Jesus Christ is Lord, to the glory of God the Father.**
> **–Philippians 2:11**

Luke 2:11
John 13:13
John 20:28
Romans 10:9
Romans 14:9

He's over everything. You don't have to wonder or be confused about who controls what happens.

Although Jesus is Lord over everything, you still have choices to make. You make the choice of what you will say, how you will act, and what you will do. Sometimes you might forget that Jesus is Lord and act like you're in control instead. You might think you know what's best and make decisions that aren't best for you. You are human, and you will make mistakes. But Jesus is there for you when you mess up. All you have to do is ask His forgiveness, and He will forgive you.

You don't ever have to wonder who's really in charge. When it comes to your life, there's no need for a president or a queen or a prime minister. Jesus is Lord, and He is all you need.

Dear God,

I thank You for making Jesus Lord of all. He's in charge of everything. Sometimes I try to be in control instead. When I get scared, angry, or confused, help me to remember who is in charge.

Amen

- Name some situations when you might need to be reminded Jesus is Lord of everything.

- Why is it important to know Jesus is in charge?

- How have you ever tried to be in charge of your life instead of letting Jesus be in charge?

- What is a time you've been through that you are glad to know Jesus is Lord?

1. Jesus is the Lord of all. Think about the word *all*.

2. Write down the words that came to mind when you thought about that word.

3. Use the words to create a prayer activity. Say: "Jesus, thank You that You are Lord of _____."

4. If you find yourself starting to worry about something, remember the prayer activity, and place whatever you are worrying about in the blank.

Following Your Guide:
LEARNING FROM THE BEST

You have a lot to learn in life, and Jesus is the ultimate Teacher.

Colin checked his compass. "This way, guys!" he shouted to the group. He and his friends couldn't wait to make it to Survival Springs. Colin had told them what a cool place it was and how the temperature of the water was just perfect for swimming.

Luke looked a little confused. "Colin, how do you know which way to go? You don't even have a map!" he asked.

Colin smiled and held up his compass. "My youth pastor Mike taught me how to use a compass when I visited Survival Springs with him and his family last summer. Pastor Mike showed me how to use the compass to navigate my way through the woods. He's a good teacher."

A few minutes later, the guys reached Survival Springs, and boy, was Colin right! The place was the perfect swimming hole.

Once Pastor Mike had taught Colin how to use a compass, Colin could read it by himself and know which way to go. Do you know people like Pastor Mike who have taught you important things too? Good teachers are blessings.

Jesus is the ultimate Teacher. When He was on earth, He used parables (or stories) to help people understand how to live a holy life. You can find almost fifty of His parables in the Bible! In one of them, Jesus talks about a farmer who plants seeds that land in three places: on a path, in the rocks, and in good soil. He uses the parable to explain what people do when they hear about God's Word. Some people do nothing. Others get excited about what they hear but don't do anything with what they've learned. Those who hear the message, understand it, and act on it are like the seeds that land in the good soil and grow into healthy plants.

Reading and studying Jesus' parables is a great way to learn how to live a holy life. If you listen to His message and learn from Him, you can be like the seed that lands on good soil and grows. Are you ready to learn from Jesus, the ultimate teacher?

This man came to Him at night and said, "Rabbi, we know that You have come from God as a teacher, for no one could perform these signs You do unless God were with him."
–John 3:2

Matthew 7:8   Mark 4:2
John 7:16   John 8:2
2 John 1:9

Dear God,

Thank You for all the people who teach me, especially Jesus. Thank You for all of His parables in the Bible. Help me to understand His messages and learn from them.

Amen

- Why do you think Jesus chose to use parables to teach people?

- How do you think most people respond to God's Word when they hear it?

- Why is it important to do more than just hear God's Word?

- What other parables have you read in the Bible?

1. Locate Matthew 20:1–16 in your Bible.

2. Ask a parent to help you read the passage.

3. Talk with your parent about what happens in these verses.

4. Discuss what you think Jesus wants you to learn from this parable.

Following Your Guide:
WHAT A FRIEND

There's no better friend than Jesus.

Emily wandered around her yard, kicking the leaves and hating the day.

"Sweetie!" her mom yelled from the back door. "Come on inside. Our new neighbors are here for a visit."

Emily didn't want to go in, and she definitely didn't want to meet any more strangers. She and her family had moved to Nebraska two weeks before, and she couldn't get used to all the newness—new home, new school, new weather, and most of all, new friends.

Back home in Kentucky, Emily could walk into the backyard and always find one of her neighborhood friends to hang out with. And her very best friend, Anna, lived just three doors down. Emily could always walk down the street to meet Anna if she needed someone to talk to. But now she lived far, far away, and Emily was left in a new city without friends.

Mom called once again from the porch, but Emily was still dragging her feet. Finally her mom came outside to see what was wrong.

"Still moping out here, Em? You know things will get better, don't you?" her mother asked.

"I don't think they will," sighed Emily. "I'm just lonely and really missing my friends."

"Well, you know," said her mom, "there's one friend you didn't have to leave behind in Kentucky—Jesus. Have you talked to Him about how sad you are? He wants to hear all about it."

"I hadn't really thought about that," said Emily.

"The Bible tells us that Jesus calls us friends, and that friendship is more important than any other. Think about it, Em. Jesus always loves you, He's always on your side, and He's always close by—you don't even have to walk down the street!"

"I guess you're right, Mom. That makes me feel a little better. I think it's time for me to pray about being lonely. Jesus does sound like the best friend to have in a time like this. I'm glad I have Him!"

"That's my girl," said Mom. "Now why don't you come inside? Dad is talking to some neighbors from a few doors down, and their daughter just might be a good friend to have too!"

Proverbs 17:17
Matthew 28:20

John 13:34 John 15:13
John 15:14

"I do not call you slaves anymore. . . . I have called you friends, because I have made known to you everything I have heard from My Father."
—John 15:15

81

Dear God,

Friends are so important. Thank You for all my friends, especially for Jesus. Help me to turn to Him first when I need someone to talk to. And please help me to be a good friend to others. Amen

- Have you ever lost a good friend? How did it make you feel?
- Who are your best friends? Why?
- Are you a good friend to others?
- Do you think of Jesus as one of your friends?
- Why is Jesus the best friend of all?

1. Make a list of the things you look for in a friend. Is it someone who is kind? Funny? Loyal? Patient?

2. Look at your list. Do those words describe Jesus?

3. Grab a piece of paper and write a letter to Jesus, thanking Him for all the characteristics that make Him the best friend of all.

Making Camp

As you continue on your journey, it will soon be time to set up camp with your fellow travelers! Remember—sometimes the best part of an adventure is the people you meet along the way, so you need to know how to treat them. The Bible is full of examples and wisdom on how to build strong relationships, so get ready. After all, God wants us all to work together on this journey.

Making Camp:
CAMP PINK-OUT

Do you appreciate what you've been given? Learn how to be content with what you have.

When Tasha arrived at the campsite, she couldn't help but notice all of Alexis's stuff. Her pink stuff. Her backpack, her pillow, her mini TV—even her toothbrush was pink. Everything matched perfectly, and her stepmom's stuff matched too!

"Mom," Tasha began, "how come we had to bring these old sleeping bags? They're so . . . so brown."

Mom replied, "Do you know how many awesome camping trips these old sleeping bags have experienced? They are warm too. I promise they will be perfect for this trip."

Mom just didn't understand. Alexis even got to bring her new pink phone with her to the mother-daughter campout. Why couldn't Tasha's mom get her at least a new sleeping bag for the occasion? Alexis came over to say hello as Tasha and her mom were getting their things unpacked at the campsite. As soon as Tasha's mom walked away, Alexis started talking, "Ugh, can you believe all the pink stuff? My stepmom wanted to make sure everyone knew we are here together, so she bought all of these things to match. It was nice of her, but I really hate the color pink."

Tasha couldn't believe it! The stuff she had just wished she had, Alexis didn't even want or care about! Alexis looked at Tasha's camping equipment and said, "I just love your sleeping bags. They look so vintage! Do you think your mom would tell my stepmom where she bought them?"

Tasha just laughed. Maybe her mom was right. She should appreciate what she has already. God had blessed her with a loving mom and a warm place to sleep that night. Plus, when it gets dark outside, it's hard to tell what color a sleeping bag is anyway!

Do not covet your neighbor's house. –Exodus 20:17

Psalm 23:1
Philippians 4:11

Philippians 4:19
1 Timothy 6:8

Hebrews 13:5

Dear God,

Sometimes I really want the things that other people have. Help me to be happy with what I have. Thank You for everything You've given me. I want to appreciate all I have and not the things I want. Thank You for Your love.
Amen

- What are some items you really want because you've seen others with them?

- How would having those things improve your life?

- Why do you think it is important to appreciate the things you do have?

- When you find yourself wanting what other people have, what can you do to get your mind off those things?

1. Make a list of five things you have that you love.

2. Think about why those things on your list are important to you.

3. Say a prayer to thank God for the five things you wrote down.

4. Choose one thing you're thankful for that was free, and stop to enjoy it. Maybe it's a beautiful sunset, a friendship you have, or a talent God has given you.

Making Camp:
TENT TROUBLES

Discover the importance of following God's directions.

Jack was so excited about this trip. His dad had promised to take him fly fishing for months. Finally, his dad had a free weekend, so here they were setting up camp near the river. Jack's dad had asked him to pitch their tent while he gathered firewood. He told Jack to take his time with the poles, make sure they were secure, and ask for help if he needed it.

Jack knew how his dad wanted him to assemble the tent, but he was pretty sure he could do it quicker and easier. He quickly put the first support pole in the sleeve of the tent, and it seemed fine. *I knew I could do it my way*, thought Jack as he finished setting up the tent. His dad was busy starting a fire, so he didn't notice how quickly Jack got the tent ready.

Later that evening, Jack listened to his dad play his guitar and sing old hymns around the campfire. Jack loved to hear his dad sing, especially when he could look up at the sky and see stars everywhere. *What an amazing world God created*, thought Jack. But when he heard his dad sing a song about trusting and obeying, Jack began to get nervous. Maybe he should have obeyed his dad and followed his directions for setting up the tent. But surely everything would be okay, right?

> The one who follows instruction is on the path to life, but the one who rejects correction goes astray.
> —Proverbs 10:17

Proverbs 3:1
Proverbs 12:1
Proverbs 22:17-19
Matthew 7:24-27
Luke 11:28

Soon after, it was time to get some sleep. Jack crawled in and headed for his sleeping bag. As Jack's dad leaned over to get in the tent, he bumped into one of the poles. The tent began to collapse around them.

"Yikes! Sorry, Dad!" yelled Jack from underneath the falling tent. "I put the tent together differently than what you told me to do. I thought I was smarter than you, but now I realize I should have trusted your way or asked for help."

He heard his dad laughing under the next lump of canvas. "Thanks for being honest with me, Jack. Why don't we make our way out and then put the tent up together?"

As they worked, Jack's dad talked about the importance of doing something right. He explained, "Following instructions is important, especially those found in the Bible. God's way can help you avoid a lot of pitfalls in life—and tent-falls too!"

Dear God,

Sometimes I get tired of people telling me what to do just because I'm a kid. Help me to be a good listener and to obey instead, especially when they are God's instructions.
Amen

- Why is it difficult to follow directions?

- According to Proverbs 10:17, what will happen if you obey instructions?

- What should you do if you realize you made a mistake and didn't follow instructions?

- How can you respond the next time you are asked to do something by a parent?

1. Plan to surprise your parents. The next time they ask you to do something, listen carefully.

2. Complete the action and follow the instructions very closely.

3. Be sure not to complain or bring attention to what you've done.

4. Maybe your parents will notice how well you followed directions, or maybe they won't. Either way, you are honoring your parents and God by following Proverbs 10:17.

Making Camp:
A BUMPY RIDE

What's the longest road trip you've ever taken? Sometimes a long car trip can seem to take forever. Maybe your brother won't stop poking you or your sister won't stop yelling in your ear. Your mom is torturing you with talk radio for four hours, and your dad is somehow hitting every pothole in the road. Anyone could understand why it would be easy to lose your patience during such a bumpy ride!

Why can't my family get it together and quit frustrating me? I really want to be nice to everyone and have a good trip. But first they have to stop being annoying!

You may think you have the answer to family peace and a smooth road trip. The truth is you do, but probably not in the way you think you do. Take a look at Luke 6:31 again. Do you see any "ifs" in front of the verse? Nope. Do you see anything that says when people do exactly what you want, then you treat them the way you want to be treated? Nope. The way you treat others isn't based on whether they do the same for you.

Think about it—God loves you no matter what you do, and He knows everything you do! He loves you even when you're rude to Him, when you ignore Him, and when you disobey Him. We are supposed to show love to others in the same way—even when they don't treat us the way we want them to.

Whether you're on a long trip with family or just trying to work together with friends or teammates, remember Luke 6:31. Whatever you do, make sure you are treating everyone else like you would want to be treated. You may feel like griping continuously between rest stops and poking your brother back fifty times, but should you? Nope. Yelling at your sister and then turning your iPod up so that everyone else in the car can hear it through your headphones may feel good for a moment. But that's not what the Bible says to do. Instead, make a better choice. Respond with patience instead of frustration, a compliment instead of a snarky comment, and a smile instead of an eye roll.

Wherever you go, think about how you treat others. Be kind and thoughtful, even when you're bored or uncomfortable, because that's what the Bible says to do. And it makes for a much less bumpy ride for everyone!

Just as you want others to do for you, do the same for them.
–Luke 6:31

Leviticus 19:18   Matthew 2:8
Matthew 7:12   Luke 6:30
James 2:8

Dear God,

You know how I feel. You know everything I think. Help me to be kind to others, even if they aren't kind to me. I want to be a good example for others to see Your love through me.

Amen

- How do you feel when someone has done something nice for you that you didn't expect?

- When you're in a good mood, how do you usually respond to others? What about when you're in a bad mood?

- When someone treats you poorly, how difficult is it to still treat that person kindly?

- Why is it important to treat others like you want to be treated?

1. This week, look for ways to help others who haven't asked for help.

2. Think about simple ideas such as holding a door open for a mom with her hands full, picking up your siblings' dirty clothes they accidentally left out, or letting a family go in front of yours while waiting for a table at a restaurant.

3. If someone notices your gesture, smile. Then challenge that person to complete a simple gesture to help others as well.

Making Camp:
POOLSIDE PEER PRESSURE

Learn how peer pressure can be a good thing.

Bobby had been looking forward to this beach trip for a year. His cousins lived ten hours away from him, so this was the only time of year he got to see them. He loved getting to hear all the stories his older cousin, Todd, would tell each year. This was Todd's last year of high school. Next year, he was going to college. One night, after polishing off some pizza, the family decided they would go hang out at the pool and swim.

A group of kids were already at the pool, and they were really loud. When Bobby got closer, he noticed the kids were saying words he knew weren't appropriate. Bobby could tell Todd heard them too. Bobby just knew Todd was going to tell the kids to watch their language, but Todd went and sat near them instead! He smiled at the group and introduced himself. Before Bobby knew it, the group was silent, listening carefully to one of Todd's cool stories of visiting Haiti and working with one of the orphanages. As the kids started asking Todd questions, Bobby realized he wasn't hearing any more inappropriate words from the group. The kids were all asking Todd questions about his mission trip instead.

Later that night, Bobby asked Todd, "How did you do that? How did you stop that group of kids from talking that way?"

Todd smiled and replied, "My parents taught me. They raised me to remember God loves everyone. Peer pressure works both ways, you know. You can be brought down in your actions, but you can also influence people in a positive way too. I didn't know how that group of kids would react to me tonight, but I knew it was important to try to have a positive effect on a negative situation. My parents have taught me to love others first and worry about their problems later. I've learned a lot about how to treat others and how to try to influence them in a good way. Peer pressure is real, Bobby, but you can try to make it something positive instead."

Let no one despise your youth; instead, you should be an example to the believers in speech, in conduct, in love in faith, in purity.
–1 Timothy 4:12

Proverbs 13:20   Romans 12:2
1 Corinthians 11:1 1 Peter 5:3
Titus 2:7

Dear God,

Thank You for those people I can look up to in my life. Help me to be a good example to others too. Give me courage to influence others in a good way, no matter what else is happening around me.

Amen

- How can peer pressure be a good thing?
- Why do you think it might be difficult to do the right thing when others aren't?
- How can you influence others by doing what's right?
- Who has been influenced by something you have said or done?

1. Create a positive peer pressure plan.

2. Think about some different situations where you might need to take a stand for what is right, such as when you hear language you know is wrong, see someone being bullied, or discover someone cheating.

3. Talk with a parent about how to positively influence others in those situations.

4. Practice responding to those situations with your parents. Think about how you will act, what you will say, and what you will do. Remember how Todd chose to respond in his pool situation, and think of similar ways to respond as well.

Making Camp:
CAMP PEACE

Do you struggle with how to deal with different people? Read on.

God made each person unique. Even identical twins have some differences. So it's no surprise that you may connect well with some people and then have a hard time being around others.

Imagine that you're headed to summer camp. After a long trip, you are hot and tired when you finally arrive at your cabin. You discover your cousin Sam has arrived to the cabin first. Not only did he grab the best bunk, he also locked the door and decided to take a good hard nap before everyone else arrived. As the mosquitoes attack your legs outside, you try to wake up Sam. He eventually stumbles to the door to let you in. You quickly learn that Sam has thrown his stuff all over the cabin and claimed the first shower each day. You know it's going to be a long week.

Have you ever met a person like Sam? No matter how hard you tried, this person was just plain hard to get along with. On your journey through life, you are going to meet people who are rude and selfish and those who argue and disagree with each other. You will also meet people who just have a different way of doing things than you do. Maybe you cheer for a specific college while your brother likes another school. Maybe you don't like to talk much, but your neighbor never gets tired of talking.

What are you supposed to do when you have a hard time dealing with someone? You have a choice. You could get frustrated and complain to anyone who will listen. The Bible says to do your best to live at peace with everyone. That can be a challenge, especially when you're locked out of a cabin with mosquitoes attacking you!

You have a choice how you react. In the situation with Sam, you may not have all the details. Maybe Sam got sick on the way to camp and needed to rest.

Maybe Sam feels nervous because it's his first time away from home, or maybe Sam really is selfish. Whatever the answer, you control how you respond to people. Do your best to live at peace. If you aren't sure how to respond to a situation, stop and pray. God can help.

> If possible, on your part, live at peace with everyone.
> —Romans 12:18

Psalm 34:14
Proverbs 3:30

Proverbs 12:20
Mark 9:50

Romans 14:19

Dear God,

I realize some people bother me. Sometimes I say things about people that I know I shouldn't say. Please help me to be patient with others and find the good in them. I want to be a good example to others about Jesus' love. Help me show love to everyone.

Amen

- What does it mean to "live at peace"?

- How can you live at peace with people? What do you need to work on or change so you can live at peace?

- How might you annoy others or cause them to fight with you?

- Why do you think God wants you to try to live at peace with others?

1. Think about someone you argue with regularly.

2. Pray about your relationship with the person you thought of just now.

3. Ask God to help you come up with how to keep from fighting with this person.

4. Write the words to Romans 12:18 on an index card or sticky note. Place it somewhere you will see it often as a reminder that God wants you to get along with everyone.

Making Camp:
FOLLOW THE LEADER

Have you ever played
Follow the Leader?
This devotion is
about following your
leaders in life too.

"It's an awesome day for a hike, isn't it, Molly? Let's see how fast we can get to the top." James was staring at the clouds in the sky as he made his way down the path. His older sister, Molly, nodded her head in agreement. Their parents stayed back at the campsite to start dinner, but they trusted Molly to keep James safe. She had hiked these woods many times as a summer counselor. Molly was in charge of the hike and getting her little brother safely to The Peak and back before dinnertime at the campsite.

Molly loved being outdoors. She was always watching though. Hiking can be dangerous, and she knew you had to stay aware of everything around you. Suddenly, she stopped. She was as still as a stone. Through gritted teeth, she whispered, "James, don't move a muscle."

"But, Molly . . ." James began to protest, but then a verse popped into his head. Just last week he had learned about how God wants him to respect his leaders and obey them. He knew Molly wasn't God, but he was pretty sure she was in charge and meant business.

He stopped, just like Molly told him to do, and he didn't move. He followed Molly's eyes down to the path in front of them—and the snake that was wiggling across it. Its long body was black and striped, and it did not look happy. Boy, was James glad he had listened to Molly! Before hearing the verse about obeying, he wasn't sure he would have responded like he did. Now he knew why it is so important to obey God.

After being still for what seemed like forever, Molly and James watched as the snake slithered away. They both let out a sigh of relief, and Molly gave James a hug. "Great listening out there, buddy," she said. "Thank you for trusting me and obeying what I said the first time. I have no idea what would have happened if you questioned me or didn't stop. I'm glad we didn't have to find out!"

Obey your leaders and submit to them, for they keep watch over your souls as those who will give an account, so that they can do this with joy and not with grief, for that would be unprofitable for you.
–Hebrews 13:17

Genesis 3:11

John 14:21
Romans 2:13

Hebrews 13:7
Titus 3:1

Dear God,

It's not always easy to listen to what others tell me to do. Sometimes I wonder if the people in charge really know what they are doing. Thank You for my family and others who watch over me. Help me to remember that those in charge of me have the job of keeping me safe.

Amen

- Who are your leaders, and what do you think it means to submit to them?

- According to Hebrews 13:17, what are your leaders responsible for doing?

- What ways can you show respect for the leaders in your life?

- Why do you think some kids choose not to obey the leaders in their lives?

1. Fold a piece of paper in half, then fold it in half once again. Unfold the paper to reveal 4 sections made by folding the paper.

2. Label each of the places with the following terms: Political, School, Home, and Social.

3. List the names of leaders you have in each area of your life.

4. Spend a few moments praying for the leaders you wrote down. Ask God to help you obey and respect the leaders in your life.

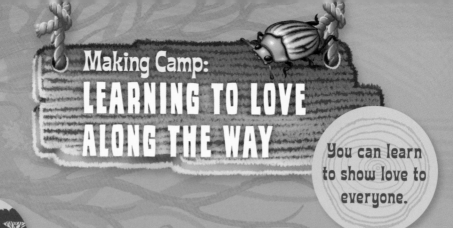

Making Camp:
LEARNING TO LOVE ALONG THE WAY

You can learn to show love to everyone.

I once spent a few weeks far away from home. I was unpacking my things when my roommate walked in. I knew who she was, but I didn't think I liked her. She was from a different state. She talked differently. She was older than I was. She already had lots of friends, so I didn't think she wanted to be around me. I knew we had to share space for two weeks, so I figured I had to do my best to make it through my time with her.

The more I got to know my roommate, the more I realized I was wrong about her. I didn't have a reason to dislike her. I really didn't even know her! She turned out to be a funny person. We would stay up late talking. I learned a lot about her and her family. I got to know her friends who were on the trip too. We would sit by each other on the bus and learn more about where each other lived and how different our lives were.

Getting to know new people can be scary. You may worry that you won't like people you don't know well. But how do you know unless you try? God created everyone, and He loves everyone. In the Bible, you can read about how Jesus showed love to everyone He met when He was on earth. He talked to people no one else would go near.

> If anyone says, "I love God," yet hates his brother, he is a liar. For the person who does not love his brother he has seen cannot love the God he has not seen.
> –1 John 4:20

John 13:45
1 Peter 1:8
1 John 2:9
1 John 4:12
1 John 3:17

God doesn't play favorites. He loves you and the stranger on the street the same. He wants you to show love to others too. In 1 John 4:20, He even says if you don't love people, you are a liar. On this journey, choose to love others, both the people you know and the people you meet along the way. If you are nervous to reach out to someone you don't know, ask God for help! God can help you make the choice to love everyone you meet, because showing love to others is showing love to God.

Dear God,

Thank You for Your love. Thank You for sending Jesus to die on the cross for me. Your love is amazing. Help me to show that love to others, whether I know them well or not. I want to be more like You.

Amen

???

- Have you ever been surprised to find out things you didn't know about a new friend?

- Do you think it's hard or easy to reach out and show love to people you don't know?

- How can you love someone who doesn't seem to love you?

- Why don't you have to be best friends with everyone you love?

1. Use scissors to cut out the shape of a heart from a piece of paper.

2. On one side, list the initials of people you love.

3. On the other side of the heart, list the initials of people who might need some love shown to them. Is there a new student who doesn't know anybody or a friend who needs help with a bully?

4. Tuck the heart in your pillowcase. Whenever you remember it, pull out the heart and thank God for those you love. Then ask God to help you remind those on the back of the heart that God loves them.

Making Camp:
ANGER MANAGEMENT IN THE MOUNTAINS

What did you just say? Think carefully about the words you speak.

Andrew's attitude was awful. All he had done the whole hike was complain. It was too hot. His backpack was too heavy. He missed his video games. He was mad that his mom made him come on the hike in the first place.

Everyone was getting tired of listening to him complain. Sawyer, who always got along with everyone, even whispered, "Do you think he will complain in his sleep? Why did he even come on this trip anyway?"

While everyone was unpacking their backpacks and getting settled in, Andrew sat on a rock and did nothing. "Andrew, will you hand me that rope so I can tie down this tent?" Mr. Kooper asked.

"You can get it yourself. I don't feel like getting up. My feet hurt." Andrew snapped back. Everyone in the camp froze and waited for Mr. Kooper to start yelling at him, except he didn't. He stopped what he was doing and walked over to Andrew. We couldn't hear what he said to him, but Andrew got up and handed him the rope.

Later that night, gathered around the campfire, Mr. Kooper read James 1:19 aloud. He asked Andrew to explain to everyone what it means. Andrew looked around nervously then said, "Sometimes you have to choose not to be mean to people, even if you are having a bad day. Think about what you say before you say it. I'm sorry for the way I acted earlier. My grandfather is really sick, and I'm worried about him. That doesn't mean I should be mean to you all. I hope you guys will forgive me."

Mr. Kooper thanked Andrew for his apology, and then we all prayed for his grandfather.

You will have times you will get angry at others. How you choose to respond and what you say matters. James 1:19 doesn't say it will be easy to be slow to anger, but you can make the choice to set a good example for others to follow. Be like Mr. Kooper, who kept his cool and responded to anger with kindness instead.

Everyone must be quick to hear, slow to speak, and slow to anger. –James 1:19

Proverbs 10:19 Proverbs 16:32
Proverbs 17:27 Proverbs 29:20
Ecclesiastes 7:9

Dear God,

Sometimes I get angry with people. Help me not to get angry so quickly and to choose my words carefully. I want my words to make You happy and not hurt other people's feelings. Help me to follow Your example of how to treat others. Amen

???

- What are some reasons you get angry?
- Why do you think James 1:19 says to be slow to anger?
- How should you respond to others who are angry?
- What are some consequences of talking while you are angry?

1. The next time you are angry, count to 25 before you open your mouth to say anything.

2. Before you respond, pray. Ask God to help you choose your words wisely.

3. Speak calmly and think about your words before you say them.

4. Choose a friend to share your plan with so she can help remind you of your plan the next time you begin to get angry.

Making Camp:
OLD ROCKS

God has a plan for how to treat the elderly.

My face must have showed how bored I was because Mom said, "Smile. Act like you are having fun. This is a once-in-a-lifetime adventure." Granny was so excited about this petrified-forest tour. It was all she had talked about! Mom promised if we did this excursion with Granny, my sister and I could pick out the next place we visited on our trip. Mom kept calling Granny a widow, and I didn't understand what she meant. The only widow I knew about was a spider called a black widow. Granny surely wasn't a spider!

My cousins ran past me, so I decided to catch up. As I passed by Granny, she yelled, "Slow down! You're going to trip on the rocks!" I looked back at Granny as she took slow, careful steps, and the next thing I knew, I was looking up at a clear blue sky. *What happened?* I wondered.

Granny was beside me, trying to help me up. Granny said, "Are you okay? I told you the rocks would get you! Why don't you slow down and enjoy the beauty around you? Have you ever visited a petrified forest before?" I looked around. The trees looked strange. They were hard, like rock. This place was different!

Granny smiled and said, "I wonder what Granddaddy would have to say about this place." Then I remembered. Mom had explained to me what a widow was. A widow was someone who had lost her husband. Granddaddy had died of a heart attack last year, and ever since then Granny had been sad. She had invited my family and my uncles, aunts, and cousins to join her on this trip. I think she needed it to cheer her up from being so sad.

I looked at my grandmother. Her smile stretched across her face as she hugged me. I thought about how much I could learn from elderly people. I needed to remember that God wants us to take care of widows, respect people who are older, and show all of them His love.

"Granny," I said, "why don't I walk with you for awhile? You know, in case you start to fall or something."

Granny looked at my scraped knee and said, "That sounds like a plan. I've heard you have to watch out for those rocks!"

In the same way, you who are younger, submit yourselves to your elders. All of you, clothe yourselves with humility toward one another, because, "God opposes the proud but shows favor to the humble." –1 Peter 5:5 NIV

Leviticus 19:32   Luke 22:26
Ephesians 5:21   1 Timothy 5:1
James 1:27

Dear God,

Sometimes I get in a hurry and don't notice what's happening around me. Help me to see ways to help others even though I'm young. Help me to treat widows and all elderly people with respect. Show me how to listen to people who are older than I am and to learn from them.

Amen

- **What is a widow? Do you know any (don't forget that widows can be young or old)?**

- **Why do you think God asks us to help widows?**

- **Think of the oldest person you know. Now imagine all the things that person has seen and done over his or her lifetime.**

- **What do you think you could learn from older people? Why do you think God wants you to "submit" to them?**

1. Think about a widow or an elderly person you know.

2. Pray for her. What do you think she needs from God?

3. Think of a way to encourage that person. Consider writing her a note, baking her a treat, or inviting her over for dinner.

4. Once you decide how you to encourage a widow, then do it! If you plan to see her in person, think of some questions you may ask before you meet.

5. Afterward, spend time thinking about the experience and how it made you feel. What did you learn about the person you encouraged?

Making Camp:
FOLLOWING FIRE CODE

Following the rules is important.

Have you ever heard someone say, "Rules are meant to be broken"? Many times someone says this right before he breaks a rule. Sometimes people use it as their reason or explanation for breaking a rule, but that doesn't make it right.

You have rules to follow at home, at school, and as a citizen. Each country has a government in place to make rules or laws, and to make sure they are followed. Why have rules and laws? They are meant to keep peace and protect people from getting hurt.

Even forests and national parks have forest rangers to protect and maintain the parks by enforcing the rules. One of those rules is a burn ban. In the summertime, forests can be very dry. This means the chances for a fire to start and burn are very high. Rules are in place to make sure no one accidentally catches a forest on fire. With very dry bushes, leaves, and grass, a fire could spread very quickly. So sometimes parks have burn bans to limit the types of fires that are allowed.

What would happen if you were camping and someone decided to ignore the burn ban? His fire could spread— burning the forest, endangering the animals, and even putting you and other campers at risk. Would you consider breaking the rules worth it?

The Bible doesn't talk about burn bans, but it does mention following the rules. God knew someone would be in charge of people and would govern them. In Romans 13:1, the verse explains you should follow the rules of the government. God knows who the leaders are and what decisions are being made. No matter what happens, God is the one who's really in charge. Unless the rules and laws contradict His Word, God expects you to follow them.

> Everyone must submit to the governing authorities, for there is no authority except from God, and those that exist are instituted by God.
> –Romans 13:1

Daniel 2:21

Proverbs 8:15
John 19:11

Romans 12:21
1 Timothy 2:2

123

Dear God,

I know You are in charge of everything. Thank You for Your power. I want to be respectful and follow the rules. Help me to know that no matter what the government does, You are in control. I want to set a good example of how to treat people who make decisions for me.
Amen

- What are some laws you are expected to follow?
- How do you think God wants you to treat people who work in government?
- Do you think there is ever a time it is okay not to follow the law?
- What do you think Romans 13:1 means when it talks about there being no authority but God?

1. Ask your parents to name some of the local governing authorities in your community, such as mayor, governor, and judges.

2. Pray with your parents for the government officials.

3. Talk with your parents about the laws you follow, and discuss why it's important to follow the laws.

4. Review the rules of your house with your parents. Make sure you know what is expected of you.

Detours and Roadblocks

Along your journey, you will have surprises. You may get turned around and find yourself lost off the map. Or things might not go exactly how you planned, and you'll be disappointed. When you run into obstacles, the Bible is clear on how to deal with the problems you face. No matter what happens on your journey, you will have Jesus by your side to help you escape every roadblock and dodge every detour.

Detours and Roadblocks: OVERCOMING WORRY

Don't worry. Read your Bible. Learn more about what to do when you start to worry about things.

What if no one picks me to be on their team? What if everyone laughs at me if I fall down during the race? What if I don't understand the directions, and I'm afraid to ask for help?

The Extreme Outdoor Adventure trip was only two days away, and Britton was filled with worry. It was like his brain couldn't quit asking questions even when he tried to stop it. His mom could tell something was wrong with him, so she asked. At first, Britton didn't want to tell her because he thought she might laugh at his worries. Then he realized his mom loved him and she wouldn't laugh. Britton told her all the questions he was thinking about.

Britton's mom said, "What you are feeling is normal. It's okay to have questions and wonder what will happen, especially when you are about to do something big and new. When I was younger, my Sunday school teacher shared a verse that helps me when I worry. Philippians 4:6 says, 'Don't worry about anything, but in everything, through prayer and petition with thanksgiving, let your requests be made known to God.' Now, when I start to worry, I pray and ask God for help. Let's pray about it now." Britton nodded, and they bowed their heads.

"Dear God, be with Britton. Help him have a great time on his big trip. Take away his worry about how people will treat him. Help him make friends and have a great time. Help Britton to be a good example to others of how to treat people and represent You well. Amen."

Britton already felt better. Now he knew what to do when he was worried: stop and ask God for help. It sure was a lot easier to let God handle all the questions in his head! Britton decided he wasn't going to let worry be an obstacle during his trip. He was ready to head out on his adventure, enjoy God's beautiful creation, and have an extremely good time.

Don't worry about anything, but in everything, through prayer and petition with thanksgiving, let your requests be made known to God.
–Philippians 4:6

Psalm 56:3

Proverbs 12:25
John 14:27

Colossians 3:15
2 Thessalonians 3:16

Dear God,

Thank You for always being there when I need help. I don't want to worry as much as I do. Help me to hand each question and each worry over to You, every day!
Amen

- **What are some things you worry about?**
- **Why do you think Philippians 4:6 says to bring your requests to God with thanksgiving?**
- **Why do you think God wants you to bring everything to Him in prayer?**
- **When is it okay to ask God for help?**

1. What are you worried about right now?

2. Read Philippians 4:6 out loud and replace the word *anything* with some of the worries you currently have.

3. Continue to replace the word *anything* with the other worries and say the verse out loud.

4. Whenever you find yourself beginning to worry, repeat this activity to remind you of how to handle worry.

Detours and Roadblocks:
THE FISHING HOLE DILEMMA

Stealing is wrong no matter who does it or where it happens.

Zach and Nathan grabbed their fishing gear and headed off to the creek as fast as their feet could get them there. Their older cousin Brandon promised to watch out for them and meet them at their favorite fishing spot.

As soon as Zach and Nathan made it to the familiar place, they noticed a beautiful new fishing pole and a tackle box full of all kinds of lures. Nathan looked at Zach and said, "These must be Brandon's. He must've run back home for something. You know, he wouldn't notice if a few of these lures were missing. Might as well sneak a few and get to fishing."

As Nathan helped himself, Zach watched. What if the lures weren't Brandon's? What if he didn't want to share them? Zach knew it wasn't right to take something that didn't belong to him. Nathan might be right, but Zach wanted to ask permission before using the fishing equipment.

Soon Brandon returned to the fishing hole.

"Cool stuff, huh?" Brandon asked as he nodded to the new fishing gear. Zach and Nathan nodded. Brandon explained that his friend had let him borrow the gear as long as he returned everything just like he found it.

"I thought it might be fun for us to try some different lures out and see what the fish liked today." Brandon offered the pole to Zach and helped him get the pole ready to cast. Nathan sat quietly and never mentioned that he had taken some lures from the tackle box.

A few hours later, the boys got ready to pack up and head back. Zach turned to Nathan and asked, "Hey, did you make sure all the lures made it back in the box?"

"Umm, yeah, Zach, thanks for checking," Nathan replied. He gave Zach a look as he reluctantly put the lures back in the box.

Zach just shook his head. He knew what was right. He knew the Bible was clear about never stealing, even if stealing doesn't seem like a big deal. Zach couldn't control what Nathan did, but he could control his own actions.

Do not steal.
–Exodus 20:15

Leviticus 6:2-7   Leviticus 19:11
Leviticus 19:13   Leviticus 19:36
Ephesians 4:28

Dear God,

I know stealing is wrong. I want to do what the Bible says. I want to be a good example to others. Thank You for all that You've given me. Help me to make good choices. Amen

- **What is the difference between stealing and borrowing?**

- **How do you think you would have responded to Nathan if you saw him steal?**

- **If you don't get caught, are you really guilty of stealing?**

- **If you take something that doesn't belong to you by accident, is that still considered stealing?**

1. Create a list of things people steal. Remember, stealing can be about more than just things. For example, you might tell the cashier you are drinking water, but you fill your cup up with clear soda instead.

2. Write or draw a reason for each thing someone might steal. For example, the reason a friend might steal an idea is because she can't come up with her own idea.

3. Talk with a parent about what you wrote. Do you know someone who has a problem with stealing? Have you ever stolen something that didn't belong to you? Have you been guilty of stealing and didn't realize that's what you've been doing until now?

4. Pray. Pray for answers and help for those who steal. If you have a problem with stealing, talk to someone about it today.

Detours and Roadblocks:
CONQUERING FEAR

When you're scared, God can help you.

Macey was nervous about crossing the bridge. It looked like it was about 50,000 feet above the ground. She knew it was the only way to get to the meeting place for the Worship under the Stars event. She hung out at the back of the group so she could be the last one to cross. As she tried to build up her courage, suddenly she realized she was alone. All of her friends had crossed the bridge already and were waiting on her.

"Come on, slowpoke! We don't want to be late!" Lizzie called out playfully. "Don't take all day, Mosey-Macey!" joked another friend. Tears started to fill Macey's eyes, but she didn't want her friends to see them. She didn't want everyone to know she was afraid to cross the bridge, but at the moment she felt like she couldn't take another step.

Lizzie walked toward Macey slowly and asked, "Macey, are you okay? Is something wrong?" Macey wiped the tears from her eyes and explained she was afraid to cross the bridge.

> My help comes from
> the LORD, the Maker
> of heaven and earth.
> –Psalm 121:2

Deuteronomy 31:6
Psalm 27:1
Psalm 56:3-4
Psalm 118:6
Isaiah 41:10

"What if I walked the bridge with you?" asked Lizzie. "Would that make things any better?" Macey nodded.

Slowly, Macey and Lizzie inched their way across the bridge as Lizzie talked. She told Macey how she used to be so afraid of thunderstorms she didn't want to leave her house anytime it rained. "So, how did you get over it?" Macey asked.

"My mom shared this verse with me, Psalm 121:2, that says, 'My help comes from the LORD, the Maker of heaven and earth.' I figured if God made everything, He made the storms too, and I could ask for His help when I was afraid. By the way, we aren't on the bridge anymore," Lizzie said with a smile.

Macey looked around, and Lizzie was right! Her friends hugged her and congratulated her for conquering her fear. As they walked to the meeting place, Macey asked, "Now, what was that verse again? You know I've got to make it back across that bridge in a few hours!"

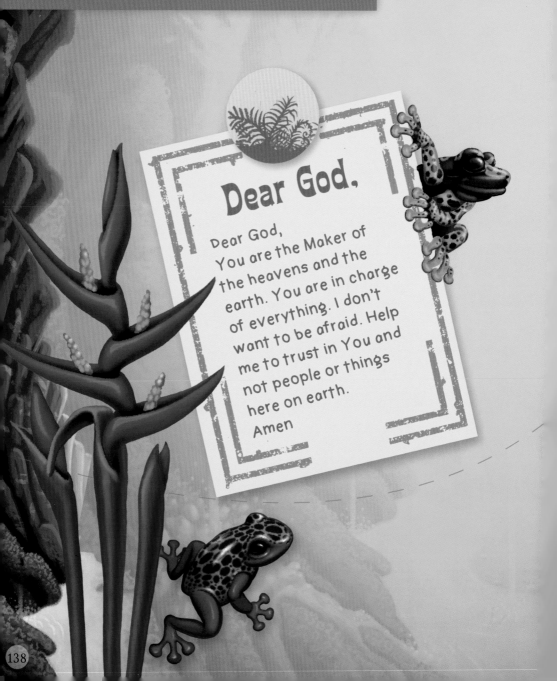

Dear God,

Dear God,
You are the Maker of
the heavens and the
earth. You are in charge
of everything. I don't
want to be afraid. Help
me to trust in You and
not people or things
here on earth.
Amen

- What are some of your fears?
- What do you do when you find yourself afraid of something?
- Why is memorizing Scripture important when you are afraid?
- How can you help others who might have fear?

1. Grab your Bible, a few notecards, and a pen.
2. Choose three of the verses listed by the compass on page 137, and look up the verses in your Bible.
3. Write the words to each verse on a separate card.
4. Place the cards in your Bible, book bag, or sports bag. You can work on memorizing the verses or plan to give one to the next person you see struggling with fear.

Detours and Roadblocks: THE DIFFICULTY WITH DIVORCE

My friend Kathryn's parents divorced when she was very young. She doesn't remember her dad living in her home with her. He actually had lived in lots of different places. When he lived close, she would go see him every other weekend. Now, he had moved halfway around the world to the Philippines!

Kathryn was very nervous as she boarded her first flight to visit her dad. She was traveling by herself, and her journey didn't go smoothly. She ended up with cancelled flights, delayed flights, and missed connections. Finally, Kathryn arrived in the Philippines and enjoyed a great visit with her dad for two weeks.

When she got back, Kathryn and I talked about her trip. "I loved spending time with my dad, but the journey there and back was terrible! I wish I could see my dad every day like you can. It makes me mad that my parents are divorced."

I didn't like seeing my friend upset. Her parents' divorce wasn't her fault, but sometimes Kathryn felt like it was. I wasn't able to really understand what she was going through because my parents were still married.

Are your parents divorced, or do you have a friend like Kathryn whose parents are divorced? Divorce is never your fault. Don't ever try to blame yourself. You may feel alone at times or not understand why your family doesn't live together in one place. No matter what you are feeling, God is always there for you. Remember that He has a plan for your life. He promises never to leave you.

Divorce can cause some difficult journeys. If you feel lonely, hurt, or confused about what's happening around you, pray. Ask God for help, and He will be there for you—with no traveling required.

He Himself has said, I will never leave you or forsake you. –Hebrews 13:5

Numbers 6:26   Psalm 31:24
Psalm 138:7   Luke 6:38
2 Corinthians 5:7

Dear God,

Thank You for always being there for me. When I am sad, lonely, or hurt, please help me not to forget that You will listen. Thank You for watching over me and my friends. Amen

- Why is it important for you to know God will never leave you?

- How does it make you feel to know God promises to always be there for you?

- How can you encourage a friend whose parents are going through a divorce?

- When you don't understand what's happening around you, what should you do?

1. Ask one of your parents for a meeting. You can meet at your home or maybe go out for a treat together.

2. Spend some time talking with your parent about your feelings. Share something funny that has happened or maybe a recent time you felt scared.

3. Make sure you and your parent aren't distracted by a mobile device or the television.

4. Enjoy your time talking with your parent about your life, and listen to what he or she has to say too!

Detours and Roadblocks:
THE MAP READERS

I can't believe you can't read the map. Surely it can't be that hard to do! Don't you know how to read? Just let me do it," Daniel said as he jerked the map from Austin's hands. When he did, the map ripped. "Look what you made me do! What's your problem, Austin?" asked Daniel.

The words Daniel spoke and his actions hurt Austin's feelings. The map was a little complicated to follow, but Austin was trying his best. Daniel studied the map and told everyone where to go. Twenty minutes later, Daniel had led the group in a circle, and they were still lost.

"This map makes no sense!" Daniel said with anger in his voice. "We will never make it to the cave before dark!" He threw the map on the ground. Austin quietly picked it up. He studied it for a few minutes and then realized both he and Daniel had misunderstood where they were going. Once he figured it out, he had the group at the cave in less than five minutes.

As the group started to explore the cave, Daniel walked up beside Austin. "I'm sorry I was so mean to you earlier. I was frustrated and angry, but I still shouldn't have treated you that way. Do you forgive me?" Daniel asked.

Austin smiled and said, "Yes, I forgive you. Maybe next time we should study the map together before we get started."

The way you treat people matters. Even when you're being bullied like Austin was, you should not be mean in response. Think carefully before you speak. You make the choice how you respond to others.

If you think you are being bullied, tell an adult. If you are bullying people, ask for help. Your parents, teachers, and pastors at church can help you. The Bible is very clear about treating people with respect. Jesus had to deal with a lot of mean people, and He is the perfect example of how to respond with love.

Therefore, whatever you want others to do for you, do also the same for them. –Matthew 7:12

Proverbs 24:17

Luke 6:31
Ephesians 4:32

Romans 12:18
1 Peter 2:17

- How does God say you should treat others?
- Why is it hard sometimes to be nice to people?
- When should you talk to an adult about the way others are treating you?
- Why is Jesus the best example of how to treat others?

1. Choose a day and focus on being kind to everyone you meet. This could be your family, friends, teachers, or even a server at a restaurant.

2. Plan to smile, say hello, and be kind, even if a person isn't kind to you before or after you speak.

3. Watch to see how everyone responds to you. If you smile at a person, does that person smile back at you?

4. At the end of the day, share your experiment with your family. Share how people responded to you when you were nice to them.

Dear God,

Thank You for Your love. Thank You for loving me no matter what. Help me show love to others, even those people who are mean. I want Jesus to be my example. Amen

Detours and Roadblocks:
DEALING WITH DEATH

When someone dies, you will experience a lot of different emotions. Read on to discover what God has to say about death.

Every time she thought about her Granny dying, it made Laura sad. She knew Granny was sick and couldn't remember her name anymore. Laura knew it made her mom sad too. She tried to remember all the good times she had with Granny. Every summer since she was a little girl, Laura had spent two weeks on adventures with Granny. They would pick vegetables together and ride around country roads. Granny would take her to fancy places for lunch, and she would meet all of Granny's friends. Granny would make the best fresh corn Sarah had ever tasted.

But Granny had begun to change over the last few years. It wasn't safe for Granny to drive on adventures anymore, and slowly she became unable to remember things very well. Eventually people had to help feed and dress her. Then one day, Laura's mom got a phone call and began to cry. Laura's mom said Granny had quit breathing and her heart wasn't working anymore.

Laura had lots of questions about what happened when someone died, but she wasn't ready to ask her mom about it. She knew it might make her mom sad. During the funeral, a man read aloud John 14:1–2. Laura found it in her own Bible and read it to herself. She asked her dad to explain what the verse meant.

Laura's dad explained, "Granny believed in God. She was a Christian. She trusted God and knew Jesus died on the cross for her sins. Granny's body is here, but her soul is in heaven now. This verse explains we should not be sad because she is not sad anymore. Laura, you can be sad because you'll miss Granny, that's normal. Just remember that God had a plan for Granny's life on earth, and now she's in heaven. That is something to celebrate, even though we're sad."

Your heart must not be troubled. Believe in God; believe also in Me. In My Father's house are many dwelling places; if not, I would have told you. I am going away to prepare a place for you.
–John 14:1-2

Psalm 30:5

Isaiah 51:11
Ecclesiastes 3:1-2

2 Corinthians 5:8
Revelation 21:4

149

Dear God,

It makes me sad when people I know and love die. Help me remember that Christians go to heaven to be with You when they die. Thank You for sending Jesus to pay for my sins so that I can go to heaven one day too! I know I can trust in You and Your plan for me.

Amen

- Why does John 14:1-2 tell you not to be upset when someone dies?

- What are some emotions you have had when someone close to you has died?

- Why is it important to tell other people about Christ?

- How can you be comforted by John 14:1-2?

1. Think about it: Has someone you loved died?

2. If so, take a moment to think of five good memories you have of that person.

3. If you can, find a picture of the person, put it in a frame, and tape your list of memories to the back of the frame.

4. When you find yourself missing that person, review the list of memories you made.

5. Remember, even when you're heartbroken, you can trust God's perfect plan for your life. He's in charge of your journey!

Detours and Roadblocks:
BIRDWATCHING

Does the Bible really talk about money? Yes! The Bible has a lot to say about money and how to deal with it.

The Amazon rainforest in South America is home to more than 1,000 different species of birds. People travel to the rainforest from all over the world to see the birds and learn more about them. The birds have learned to survive alongside other animals, and each species lives near the plants that help them survive.

Who is in charge of the birds? Do you think one person or group travels around to feed the birds and care for them? No, it would be impossible to do that! Birds take care of themselves. They gather their own food, choose a place to nest, and learn to fly on their own. If you think about it, birds are well cared for, and they don't store up food to eat for later.

Did you notice what Luke 12:24 says about birds? This verse explains how well birds are cared for and compares it to how well God cares for you. If God cares for the birds, then surely He will take care of you. Do you worry about money? God says don't. Do you worry about how your parents will pay the bills? You don't need to—God is going to provide for you. He may choose to provide in a way that's different from what you expect. You may no longer be able to buy name-brand clothing or eat out at nice restaurants, but He's still taking care of you.

Don't get distracted from your journey by worrying about money. Focus on living a holy life that pleases God. Look outside at the birds as a reminder. God promises to provide for you.

> Consider the ravens: They don't sow or reap; they don't have a storeroom or a barn; yet God feeds them. Aren't you worth much more than the birds?
> –Luke 12:24

Malachi 3:9-10   Matthew 6:19-21
Matthew 6:31-33   1 Timothy 6:10
Hebrews 13:5

Dear God,

Thank You for providing for me. When I begin to worry about money, help me to remember the birds and how You care for them. Help me not to worry.

Amen

- Why do you think God chose to use birds as His example in the verses you read?
- Why do you think God cares for the birds?
- How do you deal with worrying about money?
- What can you do to keep your mind off money?

1. Look around you at all your possessions.

2. Spend a few moments in prayer, thanking God for everything you own and all the things He provides.

3. Focus on things God has given you and not on the things you don't have.

Detours and Roadblocks:
THE BEST ROCK CLIMBER IN THE WORLD

Do you know how to be humble? The Bible provides specific reasons why it's good to be humble.

Don't mess with the best, and thatta be me!" That's a little saying my friends and I would sing to each other. We usually were joking around when we would sing it, but it's a great example of pride. You can have pride in what you do, or you can have pride that means you think you are better than everyone else. Which kind of pride do you think Proverbs 29:23 is talking about?

Imagine you and a friend are rock climbing, and your friend claims he is the best rock climber in the world. Is there any way your friend knows that for sure? Unless he has competed in a world competition and won first place, there is no way he could really know for sure. He is being prideful. What if your friend says, "I love rock climbing. One day I would love to compete in a competition to see how I would do. I hope to be one of the

A person's pride will humble him, but a humble spirit will gain honor.
—Proverbs 29:23

Proverbs 16:9
Proverbs 18:12
Ecclesiastes 7:8
Isaiah 2:11
1 Corinthians 13:4

greatest rock climbers in the world"? Do you see the difference in the two statements? In the first one, the friend is being arrogant. He believes he's better than all the other climbers. In the second statement, he is being humble.

To be humble means you don't put yourself before others. According to Proverbs 29:23, being humble will "gain honor." Gaining honor means you will gain respect and a good reputation with others. How do you want others to think of you? Would you rather people think of you as prideful or humble? Would you rather have a good reputation or have others believe you think you are better than them?

God made you special, and you can do some great things with His help. Being humble means knowing that you have God to thank for your successes. God wants you to look for those successes in other people too.

Dear God,

Help me to recognize when I am prideful. I want to be humble. I want to be a good example for others. Help me to think about others before I think about myself, and show me how to be more humble.

Amen

- **What are some examples of pride?**
- **Why should you want to be humble?**
- **When do you think it is okay to have pride?**
- **How can you show others you are humble without being prideful?**

1. Think about it: Do you know someone who is a great example of humility?

2. Think about reasons why that person is a good example of a humble person.

3. Choose one of the reasons you thought of, and choose to do the same for at least one week. For example, maybe the person you thought of always uses her manners.

4. After about a week, stop and think. How did choosing to be humble affect you and those around you?

Detours and Roadblocks:
HUNGRY IN THE WILDERNESS

Sometimes you may be tempted to do the wrong thing. Learn how Jesus was tempted and said no. You can learn how to say no to temptation too.

In Matthew 4:1–11, Jesus had fasted in the wilderness for forty days and forty nights. This means He had nothing to eat for over a month! He was tired and hungry. The Devil tried to tempt Jesus by telling Him to turn the stones into bread to eat. Imagine how hungry Jesus was when the Devil tempted Him, and yet Jesus stood strong against temptation. The Devil tried to convince Jesus to bow down and worship him, saying he would give Jesus all the kingdoms in the world in return. How do you think Jesus responded? He said, "Worship the Lord your God, and serve only Him" (Matthew 4:10). Jesus never sinned, even when others tried to tempt Him.

You will be tempted by others. Friends may ask you to do things you know aren't right. Maybe you'll be asked to sneak off during free time to play in a creek you aren't supposed to go near. A coach might tell you to lie about your age so you can compete in the big tournament. You might be at a neighbor's house and tempted to watch a movie you aren't allowed to see.

Your friends or people you know might choose to do things you know wouldn't make God happy, and you might be the only one who says no.

The Bible is very clear you are to do what God says to do. Always. Where in the Bible does it say, "It's okay to do whatever everyone else is doing." You aren't going to find that verse. If you aren't sure if you should do something, take a look at Romans 12:2. You can always ask God if something you want to do is in His will. If you ask God, you will get an answer. He promises to guide you through any obstacle you might face. God is always there, even if the people around you aren't.

Do not be conformed to this age, but be transformed by the renewing of your mind, so that you may discern what is the good, pleasing, and perfect will of God.
–Romans 12:2

Proverbs 4:14-15
Acts 5:29   1 Corinthians 10:13
Galatians 1:10 2 Thessalonians 2:15

Dear God,

Thank You for Your plan for my life. I know I will face some tough choices and temptations, and I know I will need Your help. I want to make the right choices that please You.

Amen

- How did Jesus respond when the Devil tried to tempt Him?
- How do you know when you are making the right decisions?
- Why is it important to do the right thing even when your friends make a different choice?
- Where might you experience the most peer pressure?

1. Talk with your parents about a game plan for when you might be in a difficult situation.

2. Choose a code word or subject you can use to alert your parents if you're ever uncomfortable with something that's happening at a friend's house or a party.

3. Review the word or phrase you choose, such as "I don't have my **blue socks**," or "Can you come look at my **left eye**?" to make it easier for you to let your parents know what's happening.

4. Talk with your parents about situations that might make you uncomfortable so you and your parents know what you are facing right now.

Detours and Roadblocks:
HOME SICK

My friend Jane was serving as a missionary overseas when she got very sick with a disease called malaria. Malaria is a blood disease you can get from mosquitoes. Many people were worried about her, and family, friends, and strangers were all praying for her health. She lived in an apartment on the fourth floor and was so weak she had to have help getting up the stairs to her apartment. Some of her roommates finally decided she needed to go to the hospital.

When I'm sick, all I want is to be in my own bed and have someone who loves me taking care of me. Jane didn't have that option. She was in the hospital for several days. She was halfway across the world, and the doctors and nurses didn't speak very good English. The hospital looked different from American hospitals, and the medical team did things differently than what Jane had ever seen.

The whole experience could have been very scary for my friend, but Jane knew many people were praying for her to get better. She knew God loved her and that He promised to take care of her. Finally, Jane was allowed to leave the hospital. She was still very weak, but her roommates took good care of her.

How do you respond to sickness? The Bible tells you exactly what to do when someone is sick and you don't know what you can do about it.

Being sick can be scary whether you're home or away. You might worry about being put in the hospital or that you won't ever get well. And when someone you love is sick, that's scary too. You may have a family member who has cancer right now or a friend at school who is fighting a terrible illness.

Have you ever tried to figure out why you or someone you love got sick? Check out the end of Proverbs 3:5. The last part says not to try to figure out things for yourself. God's plan may be different than yours. Pray and ask God for comfort and for healing. And pray that you'll trust in God's plan like Jane did and remember that He takes care of the sick, no matter where they are.

Trust in the LORD with all your heart, and do not rely on your own understanding. –Proverbs 3:5

Psalm 30:2

Psalm 41:3
Mark 5:34

James 5:16
1 Peter 5:7

Dear God,

I know You can heal anyone You want to heal. Thank You for caring for me when I'm sick. Please be with those who are sick right now. Help me to know how I can help people who are sick feel better.
Amen

- When you get sick, what helps you feel better?
- What can you do for others who are sick?
- How does Proverbs 3:5 help you when you don't understand why someone has gotten sick?
- Why do we still need doctors, surgeons, nurses, and other healthcare people when God can heal people?

1. Think of someone who is sick right now. Maybe she has a cold, or maybe you know someone who is fighting cancer.

2. Make a card for the person you chose, and include a Bible verse on it.

3. Pray for the person you are making the card for, and be sure to tell him or her that you are praying.

4. Deliver or mail the card to the person who is sick.

Souvenirs from Your Journey

Your life will be filled with plenty of new adventures; what souvenirs will you gather along the way? On this journey, you've found a lot to take home with you, including a lot of new knowledge about living your life for God. Instead of setting those souvenirs on a shelf, let's use them to continue your awesome journey!

Following Your Guide:
THE BEST SOUVENIR EVER

Becoming a Christian is the biggest decision you'll ever make, and it has the best reward.

Each year, my family goes on a vacation to the beach to kick off our summer. One of the traditions of our trip is to visit the local souvenir shop. I always buy a picture frame, and when we get home, I put a family picture in the frame. This way I have a visual reminder of the fun we had. Although we visit the beach every year, we make different memories each time we go. Souvenirs help you remember what you've experienced on the journey.

Your life is a journey. What souvenirs will you gather as you live your life? The most important souvenir you can ever have doesn't cost you one penny. You actually couldn't buy it even if you tried! The greatest souvenir in life is making the decision to become a Christian. You can't buy it because Jesus already did. Jesus paid the price for your sins along with the sins of everyone else who believes in Him. He carried the burden of sin so you would not have to pay the price you deserved.

> But God proves His own love for us in that while we were still sinners, Christ died for us!
> –Romans 5:8

Genesis 1:1
Romans 3:23
John 3:16
Ephesians 2:8-9

If you can't buy the chance to become a Christian, then how do you get it? First, you realize and understand that God is the Ruler over heaven and earth. He created the earth and every single living thing in it. Next, you realize you are a sinner. (Every person is, but it's important to recognize that this sin is what separates you from God.) Once you've done all this in prayer, you are officially a Christian—part of the family of God!

Jesus died on the cross for you and me. He had the choice, and He chose to die. You deserve to die because of the sins you committed, but Jesus became the Savior to the world. Because of Jesus' death, you can have eternal life—and that's one AMAZING souvenir!

Dear God,

I know I'm a sinner, saved by Jesus dying on the cross. I know Jesus paid the debt for my sins. Thank You for giving me the great gift of being part of Your family.

Amen

- What did Jesus choose to do for you and me?
- Why should someone want to become a Christian?
- How much do you have to pay to become a Christian?
- If you are already a Christian, what should you do for those who aren't? (You should have several answers on this one!)

1. If you just became a Christian, congratulations! It's the best decision you'll ever make.

2. Tell your parent, a Bible class teacher, or a minister at your church.

3. Write it down! Write down the date, the prayer you prayed, and anything else you need to remember this day.

4. If you were already a Christian, use this time to pray for many other kids to come to know God.

Souvenirs from Your Journey:
SHARE THE NEWS

In this devotion, you'll learn about the importance of sharing the gospel with others.

When you return from a trip, who do you tell about it? Maybe you call your friend and tell him about everything you did. You may have some pictures to show or a few souvenirs you bought along the way. If you had a great time, you are excited and want others to know all about your trip. If you do a great job of describing it, you may even make your friends want to go to the same place! Your excitement can be so contagious that others can't wait to see the beautiful place you described or share in the fun you experienced.

Telling people about Jesus should happen with even more enthusiasm than telling about the best journey you've ever been on! You don't have to travel to the ends of the earth to share the good news about Jesus. You can tell your friends, your teachers, your coach, your teammates, or anyone else in your life all about how Jesus died on the cross to save you from your sins.

One day you may decide to spread the news far away by going on a mission trip. Mission trips involve people traveling around the state, the country, or even the world to spend a short time sharing Jesus with others. Some people volunteer on a weekly or monthly basis to help share the Gospel with others. And full-time missionaries are people who make it their jobs to share Jesus with others.

The next time you tell someone about a trip or a vacation, why not tell them about Jesus too? After all, following Christ is the most exciting journey you'll ever go on. Ask God to give you opportunities to share His story with others. When God gives you the opportunities to share, don't be surprised—be ready!

Go, therefore, and make disciples of all nations, baptizing them in the name of the Father and of the Son and of the Holy Spirit, teaching them to observe everything I have commanded you. –Matthew 28:19-20

Genesis 1:1   Romans 3:23
John 3:16   Ephesians 2:8-9
John 14:6

Dear God,

Thank You for the opportunity to share the Good News about Jesus with others. Prepare me to tell others and help me have the words to say that people need to hear.

Amen

- **Why do you think some people find it challenging to tell others about Jesus?**

- **What are some different ways you can share Jesus with others?**

- **What are some important things you should know about Jesus in order to tell others?**

- **When is the best time to talk to others about Jesus?**

1. Look for some opportunities to participate in missions in some way.

2. Check with your local church for ways to serve others through missions.

3. With your parents' permission, search the Internet for missions organizations around the world.

4. Pray about opportunities to serve and ways to pray for those already serving in missions.

Souvenirs from Your Journey:
A SMALL SPARK

Our lives can show Jesus to others.

"Mom, I'm really worried about Lucy," Reed said. "Her parents don't go to church, and she's never been either. Every time I bring it up, Lucy says she doesn't want to talk about it. I want her to know about Jesus, but I just don't know what else to do. I really like being her friend, but I know she needs Jesus too."

Reed's mom thought about what he said for a minute, then she said, "Have you ever watched Pop build a fire before?" Reed nodded his head. "How does the fire usually start out?"

"Well, Pop usually puts a bunch of newspaper, leaves, and sticks in the fire pit. Then he uses a lighter to start the fire," Reed explained.

"Exactly. Does the fire start out big and bright, or small and dim?" Mom asked.

"It starts out with a pretty small spark and then gets bigger and bigger and bigger until it's almost too hot to roast our marshmallows!" Reed said excitedly.

"That's right! You and Lucy have a great friendship. I'm really glad you want her to be a Christian too. If she doesn't want to talk about Jesus right now, that's okay. You can still live like a Christian should live in front of her. You can be kind and joyful and forgiving. You can talk about going to church, Vacation Bible School, and other church activities. Maybe you can even invite Lucy to VBS this year. Whatever you do, let your actions show Jesus to her. We can pray too. We know God hears our prayers and will answer them.

"Just like the fire starts out small, maybe Lucy will start to notice little things you do differently. The more she is around you, the more she will see you shine for Jesus, and hopefully one day she will want to know more about Jesus too. Until then, we can keep praying for her and your other friends who need to know about Jesus."

"Thanks, Mom. Why don't we pray for Lucy right now, and then can I invite her over to roast marshmallows?" Reed asked.

Reed's mom smiled and nodded. "That sounds like a perfect way to start showing Jesus!"

> In the same way, let your light shine before men, so that they may see your good works and give glory to your Father in heaven.
> –Matthew 5:16

Romans 1:16 Galatians 5:16
2 Timothy 3:16 1 Peter 3:15
1 Peter 3:2

Dear God,

Thank You for the Good News of Jesus Christ. Please be with those who don't know You or don't want to hear about You. Help me to find ways to show Your love to others when I can't talk about it. Amen

- Why do you think some people do not want you to talk about Jesus?

- How can your actions tell others about Jesus?

- Why does it say in Matthew 5:16 to "give glory to God" for your good works?

- When should you try to tell others about Jesus?

1. Who do you know who doesn't know Jesus?

2. Make a list of the people. You can just write the initials if you want.

3. Put the list inside a notebook or book that you look at often.

4. Anytime you see the list, stop and pray for the people on your list.

Souvenirs from Your Journey:
IF THE CREEK DOESN'T RISE

In this devotion, you'll learn about how to face the future.

If the Lord is willing and the creek doesn't rise." I used to hear that statement all the time when I was growing up. I really didn't understand what it meant at the time. The saying is from a long time ago when people traveled by horse and buggy. If it rained and the creeks got too full, the creeks would flood bridges and roads, making it impossible for horses and buggies to get across. When people repeated that statement, they meant it might be physically impossible to cross creeks and get to where they were going.

What about the first part of the saying: "If the Lord is willing"? Do you ever think that way about your future? Do you wonder about what God's will is for your life? Do you worry about what you'll do when you grow up, whom you will marry, how long you will live? Well, there's absolutely no point in worrying. The truth is, no one can tell you exactly what will happen tomorrow, next week, or next year.

Fortune tellers can't tell you; only God knows the plans for your life. Your job in this journey is to live right now and do what God asks for you to do during this phase of your life. Leave the future up to God.

Check out Isaiah 40:31 to see how you should wait for things to happen in your life. Waiting gives you a chance to trust God with your future, which is a lot better than worrying.

God is in control of everything. He sees all, hears all, and knows all. He knows what is absolutely best for you. All you have to do is ask Him for help, and He will answer you. You don't have to wonder if the creek is going to rise or what will happen tomorrow. Focus on God's will, and enjoy the view on your journey through life. And the next time someone invites you somewhere, why not answer with "If the Lord is willing and the creek doesn't rise, I plan to be there," knowing God is in control of your future. That's a great place to be, isn't it?

Instead, you should say, "If the Lord wills, we will live and do this or that." –James 4:15

Isaiah 40:31

Jeremiah 29:11
John 14:1-3

Philippians 3:20-21
1 John 3:2-3

Dear God,

Thank You for being all-powerful, all-knowing, and in control of all things. Thank You for being in control of my future too! I want to do Your will and do everything in Your timing.

Amen

- **How do you feel about your future?**
- **Why is it important to trust God with your life?**
- **How does Jeremiah 29:11 make you feel about your future?**
- **What can you tell others about their future if they're worried about it?**

1. Find an empty paper towel roll or toilet paper roll.

2. Find a small slip of paper and write down a few things you hope to do in the next few years.

3. Roll the paper and place it inside the toilet paper tube.

4. Use tape to tape up the ends. Write today's date on the tube and a future date when you can open it. Place the tube in a safe place. No peeking until the future!

Souvenirs from Your Journey:
TIME WELL SPENT

Making time for God each day matters to Him.

When you go on a trip, do you need an alarm clock to wake up in the morning? Or do you just naturally wake up? If you've visited a place in a different time zone, how did that affect you? Did you have a hard time getting used to the new time zone?

I once visited a place that was thirteen hours ahead of where I lived. This means I had to switch up my nights and days! When my body was normally waking up, I was telling it to go to bed. Five o'clock in the evening was the worst! I would get so sleepy, but the locals would say, "Don't listen to your body! Stay up!" By the time I traveled back home, I was used to the new time and had to switch back to the old time. My body took about two weeks to get back to normal!

Time has a big effect on us, and how we choose to use our time can affect us even more. A great souvenir from your journey through life is to establish a daily time to pray, talk to God, and study your Bible. Some people call it a quiet time. A quiet time allows God to help you know which way to walk.

There is an occasion for everything, and a time for every activity under heaven.
–Ecclesiastes 3:1

If you stop and listen to God, He can show you the right way. If you study your Bible, God can show you the way. If you spend time reading a devotion, God will direct you. Be quiet and listen for Him. He will answer you.

Choose a time each day to spend with God, and be consistent. If the time doesn't work, try a different time the next week. Jesus stepped away from the crowd many times to spend time in prayer. He set a good example for you to follow. If Jesus needed time to pray and reflect, you do too. Use your time well!

Psalm 1:2
Psalm 46:10
Matthew 26:36
Mark 1:35
Luke 5:16

- How much time do you spend praying or reading the Bible each day?

- Why is it important to spend time with God?

- Think about your day. When could you spend more time praying or studying your Bible? Before you get up in the morning? On the ride home from school? After you brush your teeth at night?

- How might spending more time with God every day affect you?

1. Think about your daily schedule.

2. Decide when the best time to spend time with God is each day.

3. Choose how much time you think you should devote to quiet time.

4. Sign a contract with yourself to complete your quiet time each day for a week.

Dear God,

Thank You for being clear about the way I should live. I want to spend time with You. Help me to be open to what You have to say and how You want me to live.

Amen

Souvenirs from Your Journey:
KEEP STUDYING YOUR NOTES

You've studied hard for a social studies test, taken it, and made a good grade. What's next? Do you go back and study for the test again? Probably not—the test is over. But then what happens a few months later? You might find that you've forgotten everything you worked so hard to learn. If you're tested on the same material, you'll probably have to study all over again.

Similarly, you may think that you know enough about the Bible already. Maybe you've memorized everything your Bible teacher asked you to memorize. You've read the best stories and you know all the "important" parts, at least the parts you understand. Maybe you think there's no need to keep learning. Think again!

The Bible is inspired by God. Some translations of 2 Timothy 3:16 say that Scripture is *God-breathed*. Wow. You are reading words that God told someone to write down. Each time you read the Bible, you will learn something new. The more you learn, the more you'll want to know. The Bible will teach you, help you know

All Scripture is inspired by God and is profitable for teaching, for rebuking, for correcting, for training in righteousness.
–2 Timothy 3:16

Psalm 119:9
Psalm 119:11
Psalm 119:105
Proverbs 3:1-2
John 1:1

when you've done wrong, and provide wisdom that will help you become a better Christian.

You can choose to spend time studying the Bible each day. Will you read words you don't understand? Yes, you will. Will you have questions and need help understanding what some of the verses you are reading mean? Of course you will, and that's okay. As you study your Bible, you will find some verses you don't want to forget. Underline the verses, mark them with a bookmark, or keep a small notebook with notes about the verses you study.

Life will keep giving you tests. Maybe not the kind of test you'll be graded on, but the kind that will determine whether you truly love God and whether you are willing to live for Him. The Bible is your study guide to help you pass those tests. Be diligent: keep reading, keep learning, keep studying your notes. They'll prepare you for even the hardest tests on your journey.

Dear God,

Thank You for the Bible, for the verses that already mean a lot to me and for the ones I don't understand yet. Help me to learn from the Bible and use it to face all of life's tests.

Amen

- What are some of the tests you might face each day? How can the Bible help you pass these tests?

- Who do you know who can help you when you have questions about what you've read in the Bible?

- How can you learn and remember what you've studied about the Bible?

1. Think about some topics you want to learn more about from the Bible, such as forgiveness, patience, or anger.

2. Choose one of the topics, and ask one of your parents to help you locate some verses about the topic you chose. With your parent's help and permission, you can use the Internet to locate some suggested verses.

3. Spend some time reading through the verses you find.

4. Talk with a parent about what each verse means and how to use it in your life right now.

Souvenirs from Your Journey:
DON'T STOP GROWING

In this devotion, you'll learn about the importance of spiritual growth.

"**W**e need to start saving now for next year's trip to Rappelling Ravine and Rushing Water Park," Mom said, "The cost will be even higher next year."

Nash was confused. "Mom," he asked, "how do you know how much it will cost next year?"

Mom smiled and explained, "Well, this year your little sister was little enough to get into the park for free. But she's growing fast, and she'll be big enough to ride some of the rides next year. We'll have to buy another ticket to the park."

"Wow, I guess I hadn't thought of that. She was so little this year, but I guess next year she'll be ready for the rides!" Nash said.

Mom nodded her head, "That's right. I bet she'll be excited. We will have so much fun!"

Do you remember the first time you were able to ride the rides at the amusement park or ride the bus to school by yourself? You grow taller each year, and your physical appearance changes. Your body is probably growing, changing, and maturing right this very minute! When you first started walking, you were probably wobbly with each step. But now your feet and legs can do amazing things. You're growing up. God designed you that way.

God also designed you to grow spiritually, the way Jesus did. Luke 2:52 tells us that when Jesus was on earth, He grew "in wisdom and in stature." When you first become a Christian, you still have much to learn about God and His Word. Maybe your prayers remain pretty simple and you have a hard time understanding everything the preacher says. But the longer you are a Christian, the more you can grow in your knowledge of the Bible and what it means. Maybe your prayers become deeper. Or when your Bible class teacher makes points, you understand him and remember the points at school the next day.

So when you find yourself finally tall enough to ride that giant roller coaster or big enough to need all new shoes, remember that God wants you to grow spiritually too. He designed you to want to know more about Him. You can never be God, but you can work hard to learn more about Him and serve Him more—no matter how much you grow.

And Jesus increased in wisdom and stature, and in favor with God and with people.
–Luke 2:52

Ephesians 4:12-13   Ephesians 4:15-16
Colossians 10:9-10   Titus 2:11-14
Hebrews 5:12-14

Dear God,

I want to know You more. I know I need You.
I know I need to keep growing spiritually.
Show me what to do.

Amen

- **What would happen if you never grew spiritually as a Christian?**

- **How do you think a spiritually mature Christian is different than a new Christian?**

- **Why do you think God wants you to be hungry for His Word? How is this different than being hungry for physical food?**

- **How do you think you measure spiritual growth?**

1. Cut a one-inch-thick strip of construction paper.

2. Spend some time thinking about some possible spiritual goals you have for yourself. If you aren't sure what a spiritual goal is, talk with a parent or a church leader for help.

3. Write at least one goal on the strip of paper, and place it in your Bible.

4. Use the strip to serve as a reminder of your spiritual goal each time you open your Bible.

Souvenirs from Your Journey:
A GOOD SUPPORT SYSTEM

The Bible tells us to keep encouraging each other—we need the support!

"Just a little bit further, you're almost there!" yelled Brayden, "I know you can do it!" His friend Ella was walking across a rope that led to the top of the zip line. Ella was wearing a safety harness, but she had made the mistake of looking down. Now she was scared, but Brayden kept talking to her. "You are doing great!" he said.

Finally, Ella reached the platform for the zip line. She and Brayden went down at the same time. The views were amazing! Ella was so glad Brayden had inspired her not to give up. His encouraging words made a big difference and helped her overcome her fear.

How does it make you feel when someone supports you and encourages you? Being appreciated, noticed, and cheered for really can make a difference in how you feel and can increase your confidence. The Bible is full of verses about the importance of encouraging others.

Encouragement is a great way to be an example of God's love. People you know will have difficult days where nothing seems to go right. Those are the perfect times to share some encouraging words and show them there is hope. God wants you to be an encouragement to others and to choose friends who will be an encouragement to you. That way you can build others up and friends can build you up too.

The next time you see someone who looks sad, consider smiling and saying hello. Being an encourager doesn't have to be difficult. A smile, a few words, a hug, or a quick note can make a big difference to someone who is struggling. You can't solve someone's problem for her, but you can point her to the one who can, Jesus Christ.

Therefore encourage one another and build each other up as you are already doing.
–1 Thessalonians 5:11

Proverbs 11:25   Proverbs 27:17
Acts 15:32   Ephesians 4:2
Colossians 2:2

- What are some different words of encouragement? Make a list of those words.
- Think of different times you can use those words to encourage others.
- Challenge yourself to be an encourager to others this week by using the words you listed.

1. Why do you think encouraging other Christians was important when the Bible was written?
2. How do you think people in the Bible encouraged one another without using telephone calls, texts, or e-mails?
3. How does it make you feel when someone encourages you?
4. How do people respond to you when you encourage them?

Dear God,

Thank You for giving me hope no matter what happens to me. Help me to share that hope with others by noticing when people need encouragement. Show me how to point them toward You. Amen

NO-MATTER-WHERE WORSHIP

Worshipping God can take place anywhere.

When is the last time you moved to a new house or just visited a new place overnight? There were probably sounds you weren't used to hearing and smells you weren't used to smelling. If you were on a trip, perhaps there were even languages you had never heard spoken before. Being in a new place can definitely be a little scary.

In the book of Acts, the Bible tells us about a time that Paul and Silas found themselves in a strange place—prison! They were locked up for making a man angry. Paul and Silas didn't deserve to be there. However, they chose to use the time to praise God and share Jesus' amazing gift with others! Can you imagine being put in prison when you weren't guilty and then choosing to worship God? Do you think Paul and Silas were scared? Maybe they were, but they knew God was there with them. They even used the opportunity to share the Good News of Jesus with the jailer!

About midnight Paul and Silas were praying and singing hymns to God, and the prisoners were listening to them. –Acts 16:25

Are you like Paul and Silas and willing to worship wherever you are? Think about it: Jesus gave His life so that others can choose to accept the gift of eternal life. Worshipping Jesus is a great example of how to express your thankfulness for the gift of eternal life.

Worship is an important part of a Christian's life. God deserves to be praised, whether you're at church, at home, at camp, or in a strange new place. If Paul and Silas could worship God in prison, God can be worshipped anywhere! And there are many different ways to worship too. Will you praise Him with music, in silent prayer, or with words? No matter where you go, God is worthy of your worship.

Psalm 71:8

Psalm 100:2
Psalm 100:4-5

Psalm 150:6
Isaiah 25:1

Dear God,

Thank You, God, for Your amazing gift— Your Son, Jesus. I want to worship You no matter where I am! Thank You for Your love.

Amen

204

- What is the strangest place you've ever worshipped God?
- Why have you ever been afraid to worship God where you were?
- Why is worshipping God important?
- What's your favorite way to worship God?

1. Locate Psalm 100 in your Bible.
2. Read aloud Psalm 100 as an act of worship.
3. Notice all the things Psalm 100 says about God.
4. Praise God for what He means to you.

Applying Scripture in your life is important.

Afew years ago, I was training to run a half marathon. My friends and I got up early one morning to train while it was still dark. One minute I was running, and the next minute I was on the ground looking up at the sky. Everything happened so quickly that I wasn't sure exactly why I found myself on the ground staring up at the beautiful stars in the sky. My friend helped me up, and we quickly figured out that I had tripped over a hole in the asphalt. I was in so much pain that I couldn't even walk!

After a visit to the doctor, I learned I had a badly sprained ankle. He gave me a brace to wear and a long elastic band to do exercises with to strengthen my ankle. I wore the brace, but I never did the exercises. I thought I didn't have time and decided the exercises wouldn't make much difference. Weeks after my injury, my ankle still hurt even when I wore the brace. I knew how to make my ankle better; I needed to do the strengthening exercises. Until I applied that knowledge and actually did what I was told, my ankle wasn't going to get better. Just owning the elastic band wasn't going to help me heal.

> Do what you have learned and received and heard and seen in me, and the God of peace will be with you.
> —Philippians 4:9

1 Corinthians 11:1-2
1 Timothy 4:6
1 Timothy 4:16
2 Timothy 2:15
2 Peter 3:18

Just like those exercises were necessary to strengthen my ankle, applying Scripture in your life will strengthen your biblical knowledge and your relationship with God. Carrying a Bible to church is great. Having one in your room is great too. Reading a verse out of the Bible every now and again is good. All of those actions are good, but none of them are helping you apply the Bible in your life.

The Bible is much more than a fantastic book filled with many amazing stories. It's your guide to life. Don't just let it be near you; apply the verses every day. Let its wisdom show you what to do. Let its hope encourage you when you have difficult days. Let its love make you strong.

- Choose one of the Bible verses listed on the previous page.
- Find the verse in your Bible, and read it several times.
- Spend a few moments thinking about what the verse means to you.
- Ask God to help you apply it in your daily life.

1. Why is it important to do more than just read your Bible?

2. What can you do to help you apply verses to your daily life?

3. When might you need to remember how to apply verses in your life?

4. How can your knowledge and use of Scriptures be helpful to other Christians you know?

Dear God,

I know the Bible is important.
I know I should be reading
it and applying it in my life.
Show me how to understand
and use the verses every day.
Amen

Souvenirs from Your Journey:
WHERE'S THE CHURCH?

Church is much more than a building!

I followed my dad down the dark, creepy hallway. I couldn't see much, but that didn't keep me from being scared. Everything was dark. We entered a large room. Strange shadows appeared everywhere. Finally, my dad turned on the lights, and I realized where we were—inside the church auditorium! My dad had to pick up something from the sound booth, and he brought me along. "Man, this place looks completely different at night!" I told my dad.

He laughed and said, "It's because the church is missing!"

Without trying to be disrespectful, I said, "No, Dad, I'm pretty sure we are standing in the church right now."

Dad stopped what he was doing and looked at me. He said, "This is just a building. The people are the church." I had to think about what my dad said for a minute before I understood. He was right! Without people in the church learning about God, worshipping Him, and spending time together, what I was standing in was just a building.

And let us be concerned about one another in order to promote love and good works, not staying away from our worship meetings, as some habitually do, but encouraging each other, and all the more as you see the day drawing near.
–Hebrews 10:24-25

Romans 15:7
Galatians 5:13
Galatians 6:10
Ephesians 4:32
1 John 1:7

You've probably wondered why you have to go to church on some days when all you want to do is sleep late, play outside, or visit a friend. It's because church is so important—and by church, I mean the people! The church helps Christians support one another when they need it. It helps Christians grow in their faith and offers a place where people can feel loved, accepted, and free to worship God together.

Many people in the world don't have the opportunity to go to church. Attending church isn't something to do because you feel like you have to do it. It's a privilege to get to worship with others who believe in God and have the same desire to learn more about Him.

Dear God,

Thank You for the church and its people. Help me to have a good attitude about going to church and being with others who love You. Thank You for my friends and teachers at church. Amen

- Think about some reasons you've missed church.

- Consider the importance of each of those reasons.

- Realize there are some good reasons not to attend church, such as being sick.

- Commit to making church a priority in your life because you want to be there, not because you feel like you have to be there.

1. If you've ever visited your church when a lot of people were absent, what was your experience like?

2. Why is attending church important to you?

3. Why do you think God talks about church in the Bible?

4. Why do you think there are so many different churches for people to attend?

Souvenirs from Your Journey:
GOD'S PROMISES

Jesus made a wonderful promise to Christians.

P romise me you'll bring me back something cool from England," Jason reminded his brother, Brian.

"Would I ever let you down? I promise," Brian said with a smile as he headed to the security line at the airport. He was on his way to a leadership conference in London.

A week later when Brian returned from his trip, Jason was waiting for him at the airport. Before Jason could even ask, Brian handed him a futbol jersey from a popular team in England. Jason hugged Brian and said, "Awesome! This is way cooler than what I thought you would bring me back!"

Brian had made a promise to his brother, and he was able to keep it. That's how promises are supposed to work. Maybe someone has made a promise to you but didn't keep it. Sometimes promises get broken even when people don't mean to.

The Bible is filled with God's promises. Some scholars believe God made more than 3,000 promises! That's a lot. Surely God will break some of those, right? Wrong. Each and every promise made by God has either been kept or will be kept.

Notice the verses spoken by Jesus in John 14:3–4. He makes a promise.

He will be back. He has gone to prepare a place for those who believe in Him. That place is heaven. If you are a Christian, Jesus has made this promise to you. You don't have to wonder what's ahead. God has everything under His control. One day, Jesus will come back to earth. When He does, all those who believe will go live with Jesus forever. Forever means your time in heaven will never end.

This journey you are on isn't over just because you've come to the end of this book. Your journey continues, along with all of God's promises. You have the tools you need to lead a life that is pleasing to God. You've learned about the way Jesus has shown you to live. Now it's your turn to walk in it!

In My Father's house are many dwelling places; if not, I would have told you. I am going away to prepare a place for you. If I go away and prepare a place for you, I will come back and receive you to Myself, so that where I am you may be also.
–John 14:3-4

Acts 20:32   Romans 8:17
Galatians 4:7   1 Thessalonians 4:16
2 Peter 1:4

215

Dear God,

Help me to forgive those who have broken promises. Thank You for never breaking a promise. I want to remember all You've done for me and will continue to do for me.

Amen

- Why is it important to know God doesn't break promises?

- What are some promises that you know God has made?

- How do you respond to people who break promises they made to you?

- How does it make you feel to know Jesus promised to return to earth one day?

1. Look back at each of the chapters in this book.

2. Think about what you've learned from each chapter.

3. Talk with a parent about all that you've read and done.

4. Choose your next devotion book to read, or start this one all over again!

Parent Connection

REMEMBER: Think about Him in all your ways, and He will guide you on the right paths.—Proverbs 3:6

READ: Several books in the Old Testament tell us about the Israelites' very long journey—forty years long! Read Exodus 13:20–22. These verses tell us that God sent a pillar of cloud to guide His people during the day and a pillar of light to guide their way at night. Those are just two ways that God helped the Israelites. Their journey was not easy—people were grumpy and disagreeable, there was sickness and death, and hard battles had to be won. But God took care of them along the way, and He does the same for you! In fact, He sent Jesus to be your Guide. No matter how many twists and turns your path takes, He is there to love you and keep you on the right path—toward Him!

THINK:

1. What is the longest trip you've ever gone on? Did you have to pack anything special? Whom did you meet along the way? What did you learn about?

2. If you could travel anywhere, where would you go?

3. Why is traveling with other people sometimes difficult? Are you an easy person to travel with?

4. Name one big roadblock you might face as you journey through life. How can you be ready to make it through?

5. Are you good at reading maps? How is the Bible a lot like a map for your life?

6. Is it easier to follow a guide whom you trust or one you don't trust? Why? List three reasons why Jesus is the ultimate Guide.

You have an amazing journey ahead of you. Let Jesus be your Guide!

For more Parent Connection ideas and activities, visit us at BHKidsBuzz.com.